LETTERS *from* OLD SCREAMER MOUNTAIN

At a time when white supremacy abounds, this book is a must-read. Through Morrison's remarkable series of letters to her mother (who is "graced" with dementia), the reader learns of these amazing women who devoted their lives for the cause of racial justice.

> —DEMETRIA MARTINEZ, activist, poet, and novelist from Albuquerque, New Mexico

This little book is immense. It is far more than a recitation of days spent in a writing retreat surrounded by the ghostly beauty of a former girls' camp. The letters weave many threads in a heartfelt, personal journey: the early stages of Morrison's work on lynching and the long wake of trauma that lynching inflicted. Writing to her mother, who is slipping into the mists of memory loss, Morrison writes real life into thirteen letters, each "inhabited" by courageous spirits and the power of love.

> —LAUREL SCHNEIDER, Professor of Religious Studies at Vanderbilt University

Historical excavation, intergenerational anti-racist legacies, family systems, ecological love, dementia and white supremacist forgetting, place, retreat, ghosts untended and their hallowed haunting—*Letters from Old Screamer Mountain* pulls us in like collage. How could these pieces all possibly fit together? This book does in word what Dr. Morrison does in the flesh: wraps us ever increasingly (oh that last page!) in the bonds of love so that together, without flinching, we can face what must be faced.

> —EMILY JOYE MCGAUGHY, facilitator, activist, and writer

LETTERS *from* OLD SCREAMER MOUNTAIN

MELANIE S. MORRISON

RCWMS | DURHAM, NORTH CAROLINA | 2021

Letters from Old Screamer Mountain
© 2021 Melanie S. Morrison

Designed by Bonnie Campbell
Printed in the United States of America

ISBN: 978-1-7351431-2-5
Library of Congress Control Number: 2021945052

Copies of this book may be ordered from:
RCWMS
1202 Watts Street
Durham, NC 27701
www.rcwms.org
info@rcwms.org

Cover photo by Melanie S. Morrison
Photograph of Lillian E. Smith by C. M. Stieglitz,
    World Telegram staff photographer
Photograph of author by Roxanne Frith
All other photographs by Melanie S. Morrison

In memory of
LILLIAN EUGENIA SMITH
(1897–1966)
and
ELEANOR SHELTON MORRISON
(1921–2014)

Write what should not be forgotten.

—ISABEL ALLENDE

CONTENTS

Lillian E. Smith

INTRODUCTION

I WAS EUPHORIC when I stumbled upon the Lillian E. Smith Center for the Arts in Clayton, Georgia. In the winter of 2011 I had been searching online for an affordable writing residency. To find a place of solitude and beauty in the mountains of North Georgia was appealing in and of itself; to be on the very mountain where Lillian Smith wrote *Strange Fruit* (1944) and *Killers of the Dream* (1949) was more than I could imagine. Smith was a Southern white writer and activist who, decades before Brown v. Board of Education, worked to dismantle segregation and white supremacy. My own focus was a series of essays about the intergenerational legacies of lynching and how this reign of terror remains largely unacknowledged by the descendants of its white perpetrators. This would be the perfect location to work on those essays.

Discovering that the Lillian E. Smith Center for the Arts is housed in buildings that had once been part of Laurel Falls Camp was another source of delight. Lillian Smith and her life partner, Paula Snelling, ran this camp for girls on Old Screamer Mountain in the 1920s, '30s, and '40s. Alongside the traditional camp offerings of tennis, swimming, and horseback riding, Laurel Falls utilized theater productions, the arts, dance, and discussion of modern literature to awaken critical political consciousness and love of the arts in their young white campers.

When the camp was not in session, Lillian and Paula welcomed college students to the mountain for educational events and held interracial meetings and retreats. In September 1943 they invited an equal number of white and Black women to spend a weekend together at Laurel Falls Camp. In her letter of invitation to one of the guests, Lillian expressed her hope that "out of this little gathering something very fine and beautiful would come . . . to form with each other really warm and personal friendships."[1] Many of these women were leaders in national organizations committed to racial and gender justice. Some had become acquainted at organizational meetings or conferences. But it was highly unusual in the segregated South for white and Black women to gather for two full days of eating together, taking walks together, and sharing personal stories from their lives.

From Old Screamer Mountain, Lillian and Paula had also launched a literary magazine in 1935. According to Paula they started the magazine "with three ideas in mind: to find the creative forces at work in the South; to tell 'the honest truth' about everything (impossible of course); to write as beautifully as we could."[2] Both women wrote essays and reviews of new books by Southern authors. They also welcomed writers, Black and white, to submit poetry and articles that offered unflinching critiques of Southern customs and that advocated for social and economic change. The *North Georgia Review*, which was later renamed *South Today*, gained national attention and reached a circulation of 10,000 before Paula and Lillian decided to cease publication in 1946.

I had grown up hearing stories about Lillian Smith, Laurel Falls Camp, and the groundbreaking work Lillian did in the South. Her photograph hung in our family home and her name was spoken with reverence. When people asked if she was kin to us, my father answered, "Lillian Smith is a nonbiological ancestor—part of that great cloud of witnesses that helps us carry on." Both of my parents expressed a deep indebtedness to Smith. They discovered her essays while in college in the late 1930s—my father at Birmingham-Southern and my mother at Georgia Wesleyan. Like the girls at Laurel Falls Camp, they felt the foundations of their world shaking as they devoured her essays. Never had they heard a white voice like hers: a white voice calling for a desegregated South, where every form of racial violence would be outlawed and every vestige of the Jim Crow infrastructure abolished.

BORN IN 1918 to Truman and Florence Morrison, my father grew up in the Mountain Brook section of Birmingham. As the only son of a wealthy entrepreneur, he was groomed to take over the family business from his father, who owned gas stations and tire companies all across the city. My grandfather—Truman Aldrich Morrison, Sr.—was named after his great uncle, Truman Aldrich, a wealthy coal magnate and one of the industrialists who helped found the city of Birmingham in the 1870s.

My grandfather was an ardent segregationist who expected his Black employees to work long hours for exceedingly low wages. While in high school, my father began to question the system of white supremacy from which his family benefitted in countless ways. This awakening was initially spurred by the sermons of his pastor and mentor, Dr. Henry Edmonds, who spoke out forcefully against lynching and other forms of racial violence in the early 1930s. At home my father met a chilly reception when he lauded those sermons. Whenever he voiced his growing belief that segregation was morally bankrupt and socially unjust, his father reacted with rage and his mother changed the subject.

After graduating high school in 1937, my father continued to live at home while attending Birmingham-Southern College. But his family remained largely unaware of his newfound affinity for socialism, the racial justice programs he was organizing through the YMCA, and his involvement in the League for Young Southerners, an organization of young radicals launched by the Southern Conference for Human Welfare. As president of the YMCA at Birmingham-Southern, he came to know Black students at Miles College and participated in one of the first interracial regional gatherings of the YMCA, held at Talladega College in the early 1940s.

Given his father's volatility, he decided it was futile and perhaps dangerous to discuss his radical activities or reveal the titles of books he read late at night in the privacy of his bedroom: *Native Son* by Richard Wright, *The Souls of Black Folk* by W.E.B. Du Bois, and *Jesus or Christianity: A Study in Contrasts* by Kirby Page. It was also during those years that my father discovered the *North Georgia Review* and Lillian Smith. As he described it to me years later, "Finding her essays was like coming upon manna in the desert. Those essays fed my soul, enriched my mind, and helped me find my voice as a white person breaking rank with the racist norms and mores of my upbringing."

From letters he wrote while in college and conversations with his sister, my Aunt Harriet, I learned that my father purposely refrained from dating for the first three years of college. His newfound sense of calling took precedence over everything else. When lonely, he told himself that love would only be a distraction he could not afford. That resolve remained firm until the summer of 1940, when in Black Mountain, North Carolina, he encountered the fascinating and formidable Eleanor Morgan Shelton.

My mother grew up in southwest Virginia and Tennessee. Because her father was a Methodist pastor, the family moved at the behest of the bishop every three or four years. Just as Eleanor was beginning to feel at home with her classmates, she would be uprooted and thrust into a new school. She dreaded being introduced in the new schools as "Reverend Shelton's daughter," a moniker that set her apart from her classmates. To compensate, she excelled in school and skipped two grades, only to end up feeling more estranged than ever from her peers.

Her mother nurtured a nascent feminist spirit in my mother by modeling self-possession, courage, and tenacity for her daughter. As a Southern white woman married to a preacher, Nell Hines Shelton did not fit the stereotype of a demure subservient "helpmate." She had robust convictions about many things and felt free to voice them to anyone within earshot.

In 1920, the year before my mother's birth, my grandfather began his work as pastor of a Methodist church in southwest Virginia. As was the custom in those days, pastors and their families lived in parsonages owned and furnished by the church. Nothing for the home could be purchased without the consent of the church trustees. My grandmother thought it strange and inconvenient that there were only two chairs in the parlor. She requested additional chairs for guests, but her appeal went unheeded. After a few weeks passed, she invited the trustees to tea after church on Sunday. When everyone had removed their coats, my grandmother invited the seven trustees to come into the parlor. She sat in one of the chairs and asked them to take a seat.

"But, Mrs. Shelton," a trustee exclaimed, "there's only one chair to sit in."

"My point exactly!" she replied.

At my grandmother's funeral, in 1980, the pastor who delivered her eulogy kept tittering and uttering aphorisms like "God certainly broke the mold when He created Mrs. Shelton!" and "It was never a mystery where Mrs. Shelton stood on an issue." Clearly uncomfortable lauding such a strong-willed woman, the pastor spent most of the service eulogizing my grandfather who had been dead for twenty-three years. My mother was enraged by this dereliction. When she rose to greet the congregation on behalf of the family, she dispensed with the paragraph she had prepared, went to the front of the church, and delivered the full-fledged eulogy and homage her mother deserved.

In 1937, at the age of sixteen, my mother left home to study at Wesleyan College in Macon, Georgia. Her first two years at Wesleyan proved to be tumultuous and formative as she began to question the social hierarchies that oppressed women, African Americans, and poor white people. Her critical thinking was awakened by a history professor who punctuated his lectures with first-person narratives and speeches by suffragists, labor organizers, abolitionists, and Black civil rights leaders. It was not uncommon for that professor to be moved to tears as he read their words aloud.

When her classmates mocked the professor after class and imitated how his voice broke as he wiped away tears, Eleanor refused to play along. Unbeknownst to them or the professor, she had found an ally in this man who condemned the use of derogatory terms like "hillbillies," "rednecks," or "poor white trash." My mother had often flushed with anger when her classmates used those terms, but she did not reveal that her father's people were poor dirt farmers who had struggled for generations to eke out an existence in the Appalachian Mountains of Western North Carolina. Fearing she would become a target of ridicule, she hid the fact that her father, Floyd Bunyan Shelton, was the first in his family to attend college.

In her junior year at Wesleyan College, my mother was part of a small group of students that traveled to North Georgia to spend a winter weekend with Lillian Smith and Paula Snelling at Laurel Falls Camp. Those two-and-a-half days were an unforgettable turning point in my mother's young life as she and the other students stayed up late listening to Lillian read from her manuscripts and talk about the horrific costs of white supremacy.

The following year my parents met in Black Mountain. It was the summer of 1940 at a YWCA/YMCA regional gathering, and my father was immediately smitten. He was captivated by my mother's forthright, unaffected manner of speaking. She did not hesitate to voice strong opinions even in mixed company—something he had never experienced in white women from Mountain Brook. He was intrigued that she had refused to pledge a sorority at Wesleyan because she felt they catered to women from wealthy families. Above all, it was my mother's outspoken condemnation of segregation and the fact that she frequently quoted the writings of Lillian Smith that won my father's heart. As he was fond of telling his children years later, "Your mother was stunningly beautiful, but it was also her intellectual acumen and passion for justice that attracted me. Just imagine," he'd say, "Eleanor not only read Lillian Smith, *she had met her.*"

Truman and Eleanor were engaged a year later and went north to attend seminary, my father at McCormick Theological Seminary and my mother at Garrett Biblical Institute.

They soon discovered that racism was as pervasive in the North as it had been in the South, just manifested in different ways. Through their membership in the NAACP and the National Conference of Christians and Jews, they learned about redlining by insurance companies and blockbusting by realtors—practices that relegated people of color to substandard housing in neighborhoods deprived of adequate schools, businesses, banks, and hospitals.

In 1946, when their first child was three, my father became pastor of Plymouth Congregational Church in Maywood, a western suburb of Chicago. Black people had begun to move into this formerly all-white community, and white residents were beginning to mount organized resistance to integration. My parents became active in the Maywood branch of the NAACP and worked to expose the practice of restrictive covenants that sought to prohibit the purchase or rental of properties by African Americans. From the pulpit and in Sunday school classes, youth groups, and adult programs, my parents sought to educate Plymouth members about the devastating impact of systemic racism. They also encouraged members to participate in social justice organizations and racial dialogue groups.

In his sermons my father frequently cited Black authors. One of his most cherished resources was *Jesus and the Disinherited* by Howard Thurman. He also quoted extensively from Lillian Smith, who was writing scathing critiques of white Christians who defended the doctrine of separate but equal in the '40s and early '50s. In one of his first sermons at Plymouth that stressed the urgency of ending segregation, he quoted at length from Smith's 1944 essay "Humans in Bondage." She called upon white people to face what they were saying when they urged Black people to slow the pace of change and be more patient.

> We are saying, in effect, that the system of White Supremacy means so much to us, that the pattern we are living under has given us so many compensations, that we are quite willing for each Negro child born today into the world to have the Jim Crow yoke placed around his shoulders in infancy. We are willing for black children to be humiliated, bruised, hurt daily, subjected to a psychic brutality that would arouse us to fury if our white children were subjected to it.[3]

WHEN I DISCOVERED the Lillian E. Smith Center in 2011, I had been facilitating racial justice workshops for twenty years—first through an organization called Leaven and then with Allies for Change, a network of anti-oppression educators. Reflecting back on that work, I began writing essays analyzing how and why so many white Americans—fifty years after Brown v. Board of Education—remained racially illiterate and largely oblivious about the unearned white privilege and structural power we carry. Insisting that the legacies of our ancestors have no bearing on who we are, we too often claim a racial innocence that breeds obliviousness and silence. A case in point is the collective amnesia white Americans manifest when it comes to the long and bloody history of lynching in this country.

As I anticipated my three-week stay on Old Screamer Mountain, it was that unacknowledged legacy of lynching that I wanted to research and write about. In preparation for the trip, I reread Lillian Smith's *Killers of the Dream*.

For years I have felt a primal, almost mystical connection to that book. Maybe because my father read portions of it to me as a child and quoted it so frequently from the pulpit. Maybe because Lillian Smith did in *Killers of the Dream* what few white writers had done before her: call upon white people to cease talking about "the Negro problem" and own that white supremacy and segregation were the source of difficulties besetting the South. Maybe because she displayed such brazen disloyalty to the ironclad norms of white feminine respectability and named the unholy alliance between sin, sex, race, and segregation. Maybe because she dared to bare her own soul in autobiographical writing, knowing that critics would dismiss it as "unscientific" and "narcissistic." Maybe because she believed that white people could not brutalize and oppress Black people for centuries without enormous costs to themselves. Maybe because she was driven to enumerate those costs, describing with scalpel-like precision the shriveled-up heart of whiteness. Maybe because I shared her passion to name, from the inside out, how racism has shaped and distorted the lives of white people. Maybe because *Killers of the Dream* was published the year I was born.

Rereading *Killers of the Dream* intensified my eagerness to begin the three-week residency in July 2012. I felt as though I were embarking on a spiritual pilgrimage or a journey to a recently discovered ancestral home. The desire to be there was a sweet, sharp longing. But as the time grew nearer, I felt certain that grief also lay in wait for me on that mountain in North Georgia.

I feared that setting foot on that sacred ground might unleash new tidal waves of sadness within me about the recent closing of the Leaven Center, a retreat and study center in Michigan I had helped to found with my mother and my spouse, April Allison.

Dedicated to nurturing the relationship between spirituality and social justice, the Leaven Center opened in March 2000 on forty acres of land in Lyons, Michigan, forty-five minutes from both Lansing and Grand Rapids, two hours west of Detroit, and four hours east of Chicago. The meadows, woods, riverbanks, and facilities at the Leaven Center offered a healing, hospitable, and restorative environment. We purposely chose not to call it the Leaven *Retreat* Center because we feared the word *retreat* conjured up images of escaping from the world.

We were founding a center for people in the fray—for social justice activists who needed to disengage for a time from their daily routines in order to re-engage more creatively and fully in this powerful calling. The Leaven Center offered a wide array of workshops and retreats with the goal of equipping participants to become more effective and knowledgeable agents of social change. Believing that justice work is deeply spiritual work, our programs invited participants to sharpen their tools for structural change while enlarging their capacities for compassion, hope, and joy.

The Leaven Center gained a national reputation as a place that brought social justice activists together for difficult but crucial conversations, popular education, community building, cross-fertilization, and the strengthening of coalitions and alliances. In every aspect of the organization, from staffing and board membership to the selection of workshop topics and presenters, we sought to make the center a welcoming space for people of different races, ages, abilities, and spiritual traditions.

We were also committed to making the center financially and physically accessible to all who wanted to come. We purposely kept registration costs low, provided ample scholarships, and rented space for a modest fee to social justice organizations.

At the end of 2007 I left as director, feeling it was time for new leadership and wanting to return to full-time facilitation of anti-racism workshops. Neither I nor the Leaven board of directors could have predicted that, within six months, the worst financial crisis since the Great Depression would set off a chain reaction that toppled small non-profits like dominoes. The staff and board, assisted by a large network of dedicated volunteers, struggled mightily to keep the center afloat over the next four years. In October 2011 the board announced that the obstacles to continued operation were too great and the center would close in January 2012. It was the right decision given the debt they were facing, but the loss of the Leaven Center left a gaping hole in the world and in me.

I also anticipated that another source of grief awaited me at the Lillian E. Smith Center. I would be unable to share the experience with the two people most responsible for my being there, Eleanor and Truman Morrison. My father had died six years earlier, and my mother's dementia was so advanced I feared she might not remember Lillian Smith, Laurel Falls, or the time she spent there.

MY MOTHER'S DEMENTIA had been a slow process of decline that began in her mid-seventies. It reached a crisis point in the spring of 2008 when she was eighty-seven. Her driving had become dangerously erratic. She frequently became lost while driving to familiar places in the town where she had lived for fifty years. And I feared she might lose her house. The credit union was threatening foreclosure because her expansive charitable donations threatened her financial security; the mortgage and utility bills piled up unpaid. But any time I suggested she might be experiencing memory loss, she responded with rage-filled denial.

Eleanor Morrison was a fiercely independent woman who taught in the Michigan State University Department of Family and Child Sciences and the Osteopathic Medical School for sixteen years, offering some of the first human sexuality courses ever taught at Michigan State. She published seven books, including textbooks on how to teach sexuality to undergraduates. She became an advocate for lesbian and gay civil liberties, serving on a legislative task force to revise the definition of family. In 1976, at the age of fifty-five, she was ordained to ministry in the United Church of Christ. After she served two churches, she and I founded Leaven in 1987—the non-profit organization that gave birth to the Leaven Center. My mother was my first mentor in the art of facilitating transformational group process. We worked together for seventeen years before she retired, under duress, in 2004 at the age of eighty-three.

In May 2008, I asked my siblings—Truman, Wendy and Stephanie—to fly in for an emergency family conference. Our collective fear of explicitly naming dementia to my mother was so inhibiting, we met secretly in a motel for a whole day to practice saying the "D" word aloud and role-play how we would respond to Mother's inevitable protestations.

Despite our careful deliberations, the meeting with Mother was a disaster. Every strategy we had concocted was resisted. We tried to humor, cajole, and entice her into going with us on a tour of Burcham Hills, a retirement community she had often visited as a clergywoman. "Why in the world did you come up with that idea?" she retorted. When we suggested that she might be lonely living in the house without Dad, she flatly asserted that she planned "to stay put" in the home she loved and saw no reason to leave.

Seven months later, Mother fainted near her bathroom in the middle of the night and could not get up. Those terrifying hours lying semi-conscious on the cold floor scared her into reluctantly moving into an assisted living apartment.

AS I CONSIDERED the residency at the Lillian E. Smith Center in the summer of 2012, I was deeply ambivalent about leaving my mother for three whole weeks, knowing I would be hundreds of miles away. She was receiving a high level of care at Burcham, but I was her primary source of emotional support and I visited her several times a week. It was reassuring to know that my spouse, April, would check on her regularly and call with any concerns that might arise. Nevertheless, I was apprehensive about being absent for that length of time.

"You have to do this," April insisted. "As much for Eleanor as for yourself."

April's admonishment proved to be prescient. During the first week of my residency at the Lillian E. Smith Center, I decided to write my mother letters describing the avalanche of emotions and epiphanies I was experiencing on Old Screamer Mountain. She was the person I most longed to tell, precisely because she had been there decades before me. I have always known that my passion for racial justice and my work as an anti-racism educator were seeded by the stories my parents told me and by what they modeled for me as white people working to dismantle racism in every sphere of influence they inhabited. And I longed to tell my mother what I was experiencing on that mountain. After all, together she and I had launched Doing Our Own Work: An Anti-Racism Seminar for White People, in 1994. This was an intensive six-day seminar that sought to nurture in white people what Lillian Smith called "the rebellious mind, the critical intelligence, [and] the loving heart" that are needed to name, confront, and defy the legacies of white supremacy.[4]

I did not send those letters to my mother, because of her memory loss. It would have confused her to receive them. Nonetheless, I wrote them, seeking to describe as vividly as I could the buildings, the mountain terrain, and the people I met at the Lillian E. Smith Center. I also wanted to convey my interior journey in that place that had been sacred to her for so many years. And because she had been my colleague and mentor for many years, I wanted to share with her what I was learning and writing about the intergenerational legacies of lynching.

I planned to read selections from my letters aloud to her when I returned home at the end of the month. Writing her in Georgia, I delighted in the thought of us sitting together in her assisted-living apartment, using portions of my letters as prompts, to recreate pieces of her history that dementia had erased.

My journey to the Lillian E. Smith Center began on the morning of July 6, 2012, when I stopped by Burcham Hills Retirement Community to say goodbye to my mother and tell her where I was going. It ended on July 30 when I returned to see her, carrying the letters I'd written on Old Screamer Mountain.

Eleanor S. Morrison

Burcham Hills Retirement Community
East Lansing, Michigan

MOTHER WAS IN the social room, sitting in a small circle of women. The lipstick she was wearing matched her peach-colored sweater, and her hair appeared to be freshly washed and styled. It was no small feat in those days to get my mother under the shower, but her new caregiver, Brianna, seemed to possess the knack. Seeing her talking and laughing with the other residents, I remembered my mother's rage when we first broached the subject of her moving to Burcham Hills. Neither she nor her children could have imagined then how she would grow to love and depend on this precious circle of women living on the fourth floor.

I pulled up a chair and greeted each woman by name.

"You look strangely familiar," Mother said, grinning and crinkling her nose.

"Do I?" I said, playing along. "Who do you think I resemble?"

"A beautiful, highly intelligent woman named Eleanor Morrison," she said, running her fingers through her hair while throwing her head back like a Hollywood celebrity. Sally, who was seated next to my mother, glanced at me and rolled her eyes.

"I've heard Eleanor Morrison is rather stuck on herself," I shot back.

"Well, if she is," replied Mother, pointing at me, "she inherited those traits from you!"

"Let's go to your apartment, Mom, so we can visit for a while before lunch."

I wheeled her to the apartment and positioned her wheelchair across from the flowered couch where I always sat and sometimes napped during our visits.

"Mom, I'm going to North Georgia tomorrow. I'll be gone for three weeks."

Whenever I left town for more than a few days, I always told my mother. She had a right to know, even if she could not remember either that I was gone or where I was going. In the moment of my telling her, she would know and that is what mattered.

"North Georgia?" she said, looking at the wall above my shoulder and scrutinizing the painting she purchased in a craft shop years ago in Abingdon, Virginia.

"Will you be in one of those shacks?" She pointed to the small, dilapidated houses clustered by a railroad track, the Blue Ridge Mountains towering behind them.

We often discussed that painting and how she felt about it. Sometimes it seemed to disturb her because the houses needed repair. Several times I debated whether I should take it down. But other times, she found the painting comforting. It served as a point of reference in conversations about people, places, and events she could no longer locate or remember. After all, houses such as those were commonplace in the mountains of Western North Carolina where her father was raised.

"No, I'm going to the Lillian E. Smith Center in Clayton, Georgia," I said, leaning forward and touching her knee to keep her attention focused on me rather than the painting.

"It's where Laurel Falls used to be, the camp for girls that Lillian Smith and Paula Snelling ran."

I hoped one of those names might trigger a sliver of recollection, however vague. Her face showed no signs of recognition.

"I've been accepted into a writing residency at the center," I said. "I'll be there writing my heart out for three weeks."

"That sounds impressive and important!" she said.

I detected a wistful undertone in her declaration. I had seen her wince at the mention of three weeks. Locking my hands together, I pointed at her with both index fingers.

"Well, the most important and impressive thing about it is the central role you played in my getting there, Mom."

"I did? Are you sure you aren't mistaken about that?"

"Oh, I'm not mistaken." I said firmly. "You and Dad were the ones who told me about Lillian Smith. She was really important to both of you. And her writing has inspired my own, Mom. She was a white Southern woman who wrote scathing critiques of segregation and racism in the 1930s, '40s, and '50s."

"Oh, yes, that's right," Mother said, nodding in return.

I doubted that Mother was really remembering Lillian Smith or the books she wrote. I usually resisted the urge to ask questions that began with "Do you remember?" Today I couldn't help myself.

"Do you remember Lillian Smith and how important she was to you?" I asked.

"I think so. Didn't she live somewhere down those tracks?" She was pointing again to the painting behind me.

"Yes, I think she did, Mom. I think she did." I hoped my voice would not betray my disappointment.

I could have gone on telling Mother about Lillian Smith and my excitement at the thought of living and writing for three weeks on Old Screamer Mountain. But the pain was too acute. I had fantasized that we might celebrate together the shared significance of Lillian Smith in our lives.

We chatted for a few more minutes about my brother's upcoming visit. I assured her that April would stop to see her while I was gone. Then I wheeled her back to the common area where other residents were gathered, talking and waiting for lunch to be served. After kissing Mother's cheek and whispering that I would see her in three weeks, I stepped into the elevator and waved as the doors were closing.

Peeler Cottage at the Lillian E. Smith Center, Clayton, Georgia

Lillian E. Smith Center for the Arts
Old Screamer Mountain
Clayton, Georgia

Dear Mom,

I'm here! On Old Screamer Mountain! I arrived yesterday afternoon, having stopped for the night near Lexington, Kentucky. My heart started pounding as soon as I saw the Lillian E. Smith Center sign decorated with a large hand-painted mountain laurel. I switched off the radio, pulled off the highway, and nosed the car up the steep incline. Thick, damp mountain air filled the car. A wave of immense gratitude washed over me as my tires slowly crunched up the twisting gravel driveway, lined on both sides with towering trees. I so wished I could call you at that moment to thank you for telling me about this mountain, Laurel Falls, and Lillian Smith.

Arms tingling, I clutched the steering wheel and scanned the red clay banks for the stone cottage where Lillian and Paula used to live. When I saw the green metal gate swung wide open, I knew I'd arrived. I was eager to meet Nancy Smith Fichter and her husband, Robert.

Nancy is Lillian's niece. I'm not sure if I told you about her. She's an esteemed choreographer and professor who chaired the Florida State Department of Dance for thirty-three years. Robert is also an artist and professor who, since the 1960s, has been at the forefront of experimental photography. They're passionate about preserving this land and Lillian Smith's legacy. Each year they drive up from Tallahassee to oversee the residency program and live in the stone cottage for the summer.

I took a deep breath before knocking on their rough-hewn pine door. Robert must have heard me coming. He appeared suddenly, grinning and motioning for me to step into the kitchen. Their little white terrier was jumping straight up and down beside him—at least three feet in the air with each high-pitched bark.

"Don't pay Bailey any mind," Robert said, extending his sun-weathered hand. "That's how he greets all our guests." Robert wore an old pair of khaki pants and a faded denim shirt.

"Nancy's waiting for you in the living room. I'll be in shortly with the wine."

As I entered the living room, Nancy set her wine glass aside, rose from her chair, and extended her arms for a hug. She wore a tailored pink blouse with a high mandarin collar. Her soft white hair was closely cropped in a pixie cut. "Wonderful to see you, dear! We're so pleased you're here." She motioned me toward a corduroy-upholstered armchair near the massive stone fireplace. Its wooden arms were wide enough to hold a dinner plate or typewriter. As I sunk into the chair, I noticed it was positioned directly below the very same photograph of Lillian that used to hang in Dad's study.

Just imagine, Mom, there I was in the living room where Lillian and Paula hosted your Wesleyan College group seventy-three years ago! Nancy and Robert have taken exquisite care to preserve this rustic house just as it was back then. The original pine-log beams still span the width of the cottage.

The books that Lillian and Paula cherished fill the living room shelves, giving off the musky scent of fallen trees. A large, multi-colored, braided rag rug dominates the center of the room.

Robert poured me a glass of red wine, and Nancy described the other residency guests I would encounter during my stay. We talked about the recent heat wave, the thunderstorms that are bound to wake me at night, and why I should never leave food sitting on my cottage porch. Mother black bears and their babies have been known to prowl near the cottages when lured by the smell of food!

I was awed to be in Nancy's presence. No living person knows more about Lillian Smith than she. Nancy carries that knowledge with circumspection and grace, supporting scholarship that illuminates Lillian's life and writing, sharing intimate anecdotes with those who've proven trustworthy, and protecting revelations she feels certain Lillian would not have shared. The hospitality she lavishes on residency guests is rooted in gratitude for this place and for her beloved aunt.

I learned yesterday that Nancy spent every summer of her childhood and youth at Laurel Falls, travelling up from her family's home in Jacksonville, Florida. It was at Laurel Falls in the 1940s that Nancy was exposed to the Martha Graham technique. She's been a lover of modern dance ever since.

As she shared that story, I thought of you, Mom, and your love of Martha Graham. I ran my hands over the wide wooden arms of the chair, worn smooth by years of use, and wondered if Lillian sat in this very chair to read and write.

And just then it happened! You suddenly appeared, Mom—as an eighteen-year-old Eleanor—just a few feet from me. You were seated cross-legged on the rug with your white socks and saddle shoes tucked under your floral summer dress. I saw you listening intently, wide-eyed and awestruck, as Lillian read from one of her manuscripts. I didn't mention this to Nancy and Robert right then. But you were so close, so real, I could have reached over and touched you.

All day today it kept happening. Everywhere I turned, I saw you as an eighteen-year-old. Breathing in the mountain air. Perusing the book titles in Lillian and Paula's library. Watching the sun set through the trees on the western crest. Soaking up Lillian's radical critique of segregation. Singing by the open pit campfire. Walking the stone path to your cabin. Lying on the top bunk, reliving each adventure of the day with your roommates late into the night. Listening for the screech owls as you drifted off to sleep. I assumed I'd be encountering Lillian's presence here, but I hadn't anticipated meeting you in such vivid and remarkable ways.

There is so much I want to tell you . . . about the cottage where I'm staying, about what remains of Laurel Falls, about the people I'm meeting here, about the insights that leap from the pages of Lillian's letters. So much. Thankfully, I'm here for three full weeks. I'll write more tomorrow. It's time I crawl under the quilt and close my eyes.

Goodnight, Mom.
I love you,
Melanie

Lillian E. Smith Center for the Arts
Old Screamer Mountain
Clayton, Georgia

Dear Mom,

I spent a good part of the morning setting up my workspace. This cottage floor plan is rectangular in shape and open. It used to be a Laurel Falls dormitory that slept eight campers and two counselors. It's very possible you slept in this same cottage, Mom! After Laurel Falls closed in 1948, most of the cabins were demolished. Lillian saved and renovated two of them for her sisters, Esther and Annie Laurie, adding a kitchen and a bathroom, and covering the pine exteriors with stone.

As you come in the door, there are two quilted twin beds on the right with rocking chairs nearby. On the left is the sitting room with a dark oak dresser, two desks, and a large floral-print upholstered armchair. It called to me immediately. It's one of those chairs you can sink into and put your legs up. The sleeping and sitting areas are separated by a long shiny black island that spans the full width of the kitchen. I've seldom had so much kitchen counter space.

I tried sitting at both desks but neither worked for me. One faced the kitchen. I need to be able to look up from my laptop and gaze out a window when I'm stuck, musing, or percolating. The other desk faced a window, but it was too high and narrow. So, I created my workspace around the ample armchair that sits near tall casement windows. I found a small folding table and set it near the chair so I can have my coffee or tea available at all times. Under the windows, within arm's length, I stacked my crates full of books with the titles visible. I found a long, flat pillow to lay across my lap while typing.

Next, I removed all the items from the top of the dresser. I took a photo before removing them, so I'd know how to put them back in good order before leaving. That marble dresser top is the perfect place for my "living cloud of witnesses." That's what I call my friends and mentors who accompany me on this journey through the peaks and valleys, joys and tribulations, of writing. As I was packing to come here, I realized I needed to feel their presence in tangible ways over the next three weeks. So I framed photographs of these seven women and carried them with me. I arranged the photographs in a semicircle so I can see these strong, beautiful companions as I read and write.

In the center of this semicircle, I placed a photograph of Lillian Smith that was hanging near the dresser. She is sitting outside here at Laurel Falls, a towering tree behind her. Her arm rests on the back of her chair. Her eyes are trained on an unseen speaker. With one brow slightly raised, she looks relaxed but also a bit skeptical about what she's hearing. She appears to be about my age, maybe a little older. Her hair is completely white. Knowing she battled cancer for thirteen years, I see the signs of physical fatigue on her face. Yet she's fully engaged.

I love having this cloud of witnesses nearby as I write. When despair closes in and I'm riddled with self-doubt, I look at their faces, one by one, and imagine them whispering, "You can do it, Melanie! I believe in you and in the work you're doing. Don't give up. Stay the course!"

As a finishing touch, I encircled my chair with reading lamps. The only thing my cottage lacks is adequate natural light. Because trees and other foliage are so profuse on this mountain, the cottage is dark and damp. The covers of my paperbacks are already curling. I'd hoped I could sit on the porch and look out on the Blue Ridge Mountains. But tall sugar maples, hickories, oaks, and pines block the view.

I don't mean to complain. This cottage is both spacious and cozy, ideal for the solitude I relish. Except for early morning walks at the Rabun County Park, I plan to spend most of my time nestled in the chair writing or on the porch reading.

More later,
Melanie

Lillian E. Smith Center for the Arts
Old Screamer Mountain
Clayton, Georgia

Dear Mom,

I meant to tell you that I visited Lillian's grave last Saturday,
the day I arrived. After getting the cottage keys from Nancy
and Robert, I went to the grave first thing. Before unlocking
the door of my stone cottage and inhaling its sweet musti-
ness. Before cranking the metal-framed windows wide open
to let the mountain air in. Before hauling the crates full of
books, papers, and clothes from the car. I wanted to greet
Lillian and tell her what I planned to do while here on her
beloved mountain.

I followed the narrow path leading from the parking lot
to the old stone chimney. That moss-covered structure is the
only surviving remnant of the Laurel Falls Theater. It was
called the Playhouse back then. Nancy told me that when
the demolition crews arrived to tear down the former theater, Lillian insisted they spare the chimney. She considered
it a beautiful piece of sculpture. Did you visit the Playhouse
when you were here? Nancy said it was the heart of Laurel Falls Camp. That's where critical issues of the day were
explored in plays that the girls wrote and performed.

Just to the left of the chimney, lying flat against the earth,
is an inconspicuous metal plaque marking where Lillian
Smith is buried. The words engraved on it are from Lillian's

book *The Journey*: "Death can kill a man; that is all it can do to him; it cannot end his life. Because of memory----"

It's in memory of Lillian's fierce spirit that I've come to Old Screamer Mountain to write. I need an infusion of her tenacious, obstinate courage. As you and Dad so often told me, she consistently refused to comply with the oppressive norms of Jim Crow Georgia. By rattling the cages of white respectability. By naming how white supremacy weakens the minds, hearts, and souls of white people while lining their pockets with stolen wealth. By breaking social taboos and white silence again and again. All of that!

Unfortunately, there are still so many silences that need to be broken today. The historical amnesia about lynching is the silence that weighs heavily on my spirit, Mom. If this reign of terror remains unacknowledged by the descendants of its white perpetrators, we can be certain that the lies and fears that fomented lynching will continue to infect our white psyches and imaginations. The unceasing criminaliza-tion of Black men is undeniable evidence that these lies and fears are still rampant among those of us who are white.

The killing of Trayvon Martin is glaring evidence that this criminalization of Black men continues today. I can't remember if you and I have talked about Trayvon Martin, a seventeen-year-old African American high school student who was murdered a few months ago in Florida. He was walking at night, returning to the home of his father's fian-cée after purchasing a can of iced tea and a bag of Skittles at a nearby convenience store. A neighborhood watch person, named George Zimmerman, thought he looked suspicious and called the police, saying there had been break-ins recently in his gated neighborhood and now there was a guy walking in the neighborhood, wearing a hoodie, looking suspicious and acting like he might be on drugs. Zimmerman followed Trayvon and accosted him. A scuffle ensued, and although Trayvon was unarmed, Zimmerman shot and killed him.

If Trayvon had been a white teenager walking in that neighborhood, he would not have been viewed as suspicious. Or presumed to be on drugs. Or seen as a potential vandal. Had he been white, he would not have been followed, accosted, and murdered. Certainly the murderer would not have been set free by the white police officers who questioned him that night.

With great ambivalence, I've been studying the images in *Without Sanctuary: Lynching Photography in America*. I don't want to look at these photographs. The desecrating violence is horrific to behold. But I also don't want to look away. Those of us who are white need to grapple with the fact that photographs were taken at these lynchings. And those photographs were often made into postcards and sold as souvenirs. The faces of the white people gathered at those lynchings are haunting. Many are smiling into the camera or hurling epithets at the brutalized body that sways lifelessly from the tree limb.

Some people have children in their arms or on their shoulders. I've been searching for an article, book, or dissertation that talks about the trauma endured by white children who were taken to a lynching by their parents. But I've found nothing written about this.

I've got so many questions, Mom. What were those children feeling? What were they told? What did they do when fear, horror, or nausea overcame them while their parents were smiling and cheering? How in the world did they ever access their feelings later when silence fell like a heavy curtain? How did that experience shape the men and women they became? And why do so few of us who are white ever ask these questions?

Sixty-five years ago Lillian broke this silence in *Killers of the Dream* when she described how Southern white children learned to accept the poisonous, irrational, and spiritually suffocating contradictions of white supremacy:

> One day, sometime during your childhood or adolescence, a Negro was lynched in your county or the one next to yours. A human being was burned or hanged from a tree and you knew it had happened. But no one publicly condemned it and always the murderers went free. And afterward, maybe weeks or months or years afterward, you sat casually in the drugstore with one of those murderers and drank a Coke he casually paid for. A "nice white girl" could do that but she would have been run out of town or perhaps killed had she drunk a Coke with the young Negro doctor who was devoting his life in service to his people.[5]

Lillian broke the silence by talking candidly with the girls at Laurel Falls about the horror and brutalization of lynching. And then, in the *Laurel Leaf Newsletter*, she informed the girls' parents about the tough issues they were tackling.

I just learned that in 1946, while Laurel Falls Camp was in session, a mob of white people in Monroe, Georgia pulled two Black couples from their car, beat them, took them to the river and riddled their bodies with bullets. The victims were George Dorsey, Mae Murray Dorsey, Dorothy Dorsey Malcom, and Roger Malcom.

In *Laurel Leaf*, Lillian tells the parents that she and the girls had extensive discussions about the Monroe lynching and the campers asked many difficult questions: "They want to know especially if the women who were lynched had children, and how those children are feeling, and who are looking after them; and how they must feel about living in America… and how can they feel good toward white people when white people have done these dreadful things to their mothers."[6]

I imagine some of the parents were squirming and others were enraged when Lillian challenged them to speak candidly with their daughters about the violence that segregation and white supremacy foment. She didn't tiptoe around the subject, Mom. In no uncertain terms she warned the parents that their children would fail to thrive as long as white supremacy continued to go unchecked: "They can't grow very much if we surround them with fears and dreads and feelings of superiority and taboos that shut other human beings away from them."[7]

When I found Lillian's grave, I knelt in the moss in front of the plaque. A small ray of late afternoon sun filtered through the nearby trees, illuminating the first three letters of her name. Tracing those letters, I could hear the tender cadence in Nancy's voice when she speaks of "Lil." I brushed some pebbles from the marker and spoke aloud, quite certain Lillian was listening.

"I'm here for three weeks of solitude and writing. I hope to make you proud."

I'm so grateful to be on this mountain, Mom.

Love,
Melanie

Lillian E. Smith Center for the Arts
Old Screamer Mountain
Clayton, Georgia

Dear Mom,

I'm sitting on the porch of my cottage. A fierce thunderstorm just swept over the mountain and forced me inside for about an hour. The lightning strikes seemed way too close! Now, I'm back on the porch. The heavy rains have stopped, and I can spot patches of sunlight in the coal black sky. I like to sit here in the early evening and read.

I've been rereading *How Am I to Be Heard?: Letters of Lillian Smith*. I know you have read these letters, because I have the book you bought in December 1993, just months after they were published.

April and I read Lillian's letters aloud to each other one summer a few years back. I loved doing that with April. We'd read a few letters, pause, and share our reactions. It's a whole new experience reading them here on this mountain where Lillian wrote them. Lillian once wrote to a camper's mother, expressing her ardent hope that Laurel Falls Camp will help awaken "the little sleeping beauties that our Anglo-American culture has anesthetized, or rather put in a deep freeze."[8]

Mom, I wonder if that's how you'd describe the eighteen-year-old Eleanor who came to Laurel Falls Camp. From what you've told me, you'd already begun to chafe against the confining conventions of white Southern womanhood by your junior year at Wesleyan. So, probably not.

But I do remember you describing the vivid impression Lillian and Paula made on you: two women, living creative and productive lives, independent of men. That was something you had never experienced before. You were in awe that two women could be managing a camp for girls, publishing a magazine, writing books, corresponding with Eleanor Roosevelt and Richard Wright, and participating in movements for racial justice.

I've had trouble sleeping the last two nights, Mom. The violence and desecration in those lynching photographs wake me in the middle of the night. And being on this land, rereading Lillian's letters, has unleashed new waves of grief about the closing of the Leaven Center. I guess that shouldn't surprise me. So many memories of Leaven events are rekindled as I read Lillian's recollections of Laurel Falls. And it's only been five months since we gathered to say goodbye to the Leaven Center. But I feel ambushed by the severity and rawness of the pain.

Sometimes, Mom, it's hard for me to remember why I left as director four years ago. It's hard to remember how utterly exhausted I was. Especially when grief overtakes me like it did last night. I called April, sobbing, and asked her to tell me one more time why we decided to leave. It was excruciating to watch helplessly as the Leaven Center languished for months on life support before dying.

It's good to be writing this to you. And I suppose it's good to be feeling all of it again in this place that has seen its own abundance of change and loss. But it hurts like hell.

Good night,
Melanie

Lillian E. Smith Center for the Arts
Old Screamer Mountain
Clayton, Georgia

Dear Mom,

I took a long walk this morning—almost six miles up and down the Rabun County Park road that winds around a fairly steep hill. I always take my little Sony voice recorder with me because I've discovered that early morning walks are the most generative time for my writing process. I don't have to exert any mental effort whatsoever. It's like my feet do the remembering and the pondering for me as I listen to ducks squabbling at the edge of a nearby pond and peer into the pine forests that line the park road. New ideas and startling connections bubble up. I record it all as I walk. When I get back to my cottage, I transcribe everything and follow where those prompts lead me.

After that walk I spent most of the day working on an essay that I want to tell you about. I'm trying to describe the pernicious intergenerational silence about lynching that is so pervasive in white families and communities.

In my experience that silence is ubiquitous. I know white people who have discovered that their ancestors were slaveholders. I know white people who have uncovered the fact that some of their family members were actively involved in the Ku Klux Klan or the White Citizens Council. But I can count on one hand the white people I know who have talked about family stories related to lynching.

This silence is particularly striking when I consider that you and I led intensive trainings for years attended by hundreds of white people who strive to be anti-racist allies. If ever there were a context where white people might be inclined to reveal such stories, then the Doing Our Own Work seminars would be it. But I don't remember a lynching-related story ever being shared. I wish I could talk with you about this, to check whether I am remembering this accurately.

This silence is also striking because lynchings could draw hundreds, sometimes thousands, of "spectators." I've been reading about a 1916 lynching in Waco, Texas, that drew fifteen thousand white people. Ten thousand people witnessed the 1921 lynching of three Black men in Duluth, Minnesota. Mathematically speaking, these statistics implicate a lot of white families—at the very least, white families with ancestral roots that reach back into Reconstruction or the Jim Crow era.

I've been reading *On the Courthouse Lawn: Confronting the Legacy of Lynching in the Twenty-First Century* by Sherrilyn Ifill, a law professor at the University of Maryland. It's an incredibly important book and I'm learning so much from her. Twenty years ago she investigated two lynchings that took place on the Eastern Shore of Maryland, one in 1931 and the other in 1933. She interviewed residents of Salisbury and Princess Anne where the lynchings occurred. The Black and white residents she interviewed had radically different memories of the lynchings. Even though six decades had passed, Black residents could recall in vivid detail events surrounding the lynchings. Many Black people could tell her about a family member who heard the horrific sounds emanating from the site of the lynching or saw the body the next day. But the white people she interviewed consistently said they knew very little about the lynchings, and with very few exceptions, white residents of Salisbury and Princess Anne insisted the lynchers were from "out of town."

In 1931 Salisbury had nine thousand white residents. By all accounts, between five hundred and one thousand white people personally witnessed some part of the lynching of Matthew Williams on Salisbury's courthouse lawn. Ifill says, "This means that perhaps ten percent of the town's white population saw the lynching. Yet sixty-eight years later, when I talked with residents, very few whites admitted that they or their families had any personal recollection of the lynching. And so this event, which had constituted a defining racial moment in the Black community, had virtually no contemporary significance for whites."9

I am learning that many lynchings were not isolated events shrouded in secrecy. Word of the impending violence spread through white communities, and in the aftermath, photographs, postcards, relics, and newspaper reports purposely guaranteed that every member of the community would be given the opportunity to be a spectator. But white people rarely intervened—before, during, or after—to help quell the frenzy. Nor did they demand that perpetrators be brought to justice.

Ifill notes that the Black people she interviewed on the Eastern Shore weren't focused on the instigators. Their minds were fixed on the thousands of white people who watched, stood by, or later learned about the lynching and did nothing. As Ifill says, "For many blacks on the Shore, this was the lesson of lynching passed down from generation to generation: ordinary whites were not to be trusted."[10]

What lessons of lynching have we—as white people—passed down from generation to generation? I wouldn't call these things "lessons," but we've passed down a whole lot of silence, repression, ignorance, and denial.

Besides this collective forgetting, I'm firmly convinced that we are passing down an unexamined, deeply entrenched, fear of Black people that has its historical roots in the lies that fomented lynching. If we refuse to examine the power of this unconscious legacy, insisting that racism is "behind us" and there is "no need to stir up an ugly past," we will continue to manifest the racist assumptions that supported lynching. We see evidence on every hand that this is true. We have only to consider the staggering number of *unarmed* Black men killed by police or security guards in recent years because the officers insisted they "feared for their lives."

We must break the silence about lynching and what our white ancestors witnessed or perpetrated. A naming and accountability must begin. As Sherrilyn Ifill says, "It is in the telling and hearing of formerly silenced stories that communities can re-create themselves."

It's been a long day, but I'm glad to make headway on the work I hope to accomplish here.

Love,
Melanie

I STOPPED BY the Common Room to talk with Nancy Fichter this morning. She was in the kitchen preparing for a dinner meeting. The welcome aroma of freshly brewed coffee filled the kitchen. Nancy sat perched on a stool at the kitchen counter, wearing an apron to protect her crisp peach-colored blouse and white slacks. A single strand of blue-grey stones graced her neck.

She asked how my writing was coming along. I told her how grateful I was to be on this mountain—that rereading Lillian's letters and essays helped fortify me to write about the history of lynching. Nancy invited me to pull up a chair and sit with her awhile.

"I'm ready for a break," she said, setting aside the tomatoes she was slicing. "The sweet potato pies are in the oven. And the hors d'oeuvres won't take but a minute to make."

"Are you sure?" I asked, not wanting to be a nuisance. Nancy nodded and asked how I was taking care of myself while delving into such difficult history. I told her about my "cloud of witnesses" with the photo of Lillian in the center.

"I feel held and upheld by those women," I said. "When I'm feeling overwhelmed or disheartened, I look at their faces and remember that I'm not alone."

Nancy leaned toward me, her eyes narrowed.

"Even when you're not alone, it can be very lonely," she said. "Lil had Paula. She had friends near and far. She corresponded daily with people who expressed love and support. Still, she battled loneliness."

"I know she did," I said. "I've been hearing that struggle with loneliness in her letters."

Nancy nodded and paused for a few seconds before continuing.

"I think that kind of loneliness is unavoidable, Melanie. When you're excavating the deep interior terrain as you're doing and as Lil did, it's a cold corridor that you walk. Sometimes you have to walk it alone."

For a brief moment, I could swear the temperature in the room dipped. Nancy was listening so carefully and naming with loving precision what I had been feeling, I decided to tell her how being on this land had opened the floodgates for more grieving about the Leaven Center.

Nancy could identify with my pain and uncertainty. She shared that she and Robert were in conversation with administrators at a nearby college, discussing the possibility of the college assuming stewardship of the Lillian E. Smith Center.

"That's huge," I exclaimed. "How are you feeling about all of this?"

Nancy paused. Only the hum of the refrigerator could be heard.

"There are so many feelings at once. I'm in my eighties now. We can't keep up the pace of coming here every year. We are relieved to find an institution of their caliber that will honor and safeguard the Lillian E. Smith Center history while creating something new."

Nancy paused again and stared at the kitchen shelves to the right of the door. Dozens of wine glasses stood three rows deep, each sparkling glass perfectly equidistant from the others. I wondered whether Nancy herself had arranged those shelves with such exactitude and care. She turned back toward me and her voice dropped noticeably.

"There's also sadness. This place has been central to my life since I was a child. It's been an enormous gift to spend our summers here, hosting such an amazing array of talented writers and artists."

"Will you continue to come during the summer residencies?" I asked.

Grief and a twinge of dread rose in me. I knew that Robert and Nancy were showing wisdom and grace in letting go. But I was not yet ready to imagine being here without them.

"We'll have to work out that delicate balance over time." She leaned back and folded her arms. "The college president has said our continued presence would be a gift. But we don't want to be intrusive or stand in the way of change."

"That struggle is a familiar one," I said. "How to stay connected to something you've helped birth without interfering or hovering."

Nancy and I sat in that kitchen for maybe an hour, sharing stories of transition, loss, and hoped-for resurrections. Before our conversation ended, I told her how my mother appeared to me in their living room that first afternoon and how I kept encountering her spirit in this place.

"I have decided to write letters to my mother. I'll read excerpts to her when I get back home."

"You're not the first person to experience that this place

is inhabited by ghosts," Nancy said, glancing to see my reaction.

"In-ha-bi-ted," she repeated, stressing every consonant. "Not haunted. Inhabited is a good thing."

"Yes," I said. "It's been a very good thing to share this experience with my mother."

∽

FRIDAY, JULY 20, 2012
Lillian E. Smith Center for the Arts
Old Screamer Mountain
Clayton, Georgia

Dear Mom,

April tells me it's going to be 104 degrees today in East Lansing! I'm sorry to hear that the heat wave continues unabated. I know it keeps you from going outside and enjoying those magnificent gardens at Burcham Hills. Sitting by the pond and watching the birds flit from rock to flower to tree is one of the things I love to do most with you, Mom.

I don't mean to rub it in, but the temperature here in the Georgia mountains has been surprisingly temperate. For one thing, the daily rain cools things off. As you know, thunderstorms in the Blue Ridge Mountains can move in suddenly and dramatically and then be followed by clear skies within minutes. Right now as I write you from my front porch, there is thunder to the north and the south of us, but the noonday sun is shining brightly.

On my walk this morning, I was reflecting on why I feel such urgency about this writing I've been doing. I love my Allies for Change work, but if it were financially possible to take a year and do nothing but write, I'd do it in a heartbeat. I'm already experiencing anticipatory grief about leaving on Sunday. Once back, my writing will have to be put on hold for weeks—maybe months—because of other demands. When I'm able to pick it up again, I fear it will take days, if not weeks, to reorient and recover the focus I've found on this mountain.

Being sixty-three contributes to the urgency I feel. Since turning sixty, mortality seems to lurk around every corner, appearing suddenly, leaving me shaken and grieving but also sparking in me a fierce resolve.

There's one other source for my urgency that's harder to name. I fear that dementia may be in my future and its onset may not be all that far off. I'm three years shy of the age you were when we started Leaven in 1987. At age sixty-six, you were a gifted and innovative facilitator of transformative group process. I learned so much as your apprentice, watching you lead with suppleness and strength.

But, Mom, within seven years I was seeing signs that you were struggling with memory loss, although at first I didn't want to acknowledge this any more than you did. Your dementia worsened at such a slow pace I was tempted to retreat into denial. I seized on other reasons to explain why you so often became confused and disoriented. When I couldn't any longer ignore what was happening, I hesitated to be candid with you. I feared your disavowal and anger.

So I assumed more and more responsibility in the work we did together, until that became untenable and I had to be honest with you.

We went through an excruciating time when I finally named your memory loss in 2004 and described how it was negatively affecting our facilitation of groups. You accused me of making "unsubstantiated accusations." I didn't want to inflict further pain by offering examples, but you kept pressing me for "evidence." When you retired from Leaven at age eighty-four, you blamed me for your departure, steadfastly refusing to acknowledge any loss of capacity.

How we got through that impasse, I'm still not sure. I often wondered what you were feeling, but we didn't talk about your retirement or dementia after that. I don't know if it was grace, your need for my help, or my need for your love. But somehow, with the passage of time, we found our way back to each other.

The pain of that time returned as I imagined writing you about my dread of dementia. But it isn't you I fear telling now. I seldom find the courage to name this dread to anyone, even myself. I want to name it because I don't want to later feel regret that I postponed writing until it was too late. I want to say it to you because this, too, may be something we share. And it's also true that the grace of dementia has granted us these last few years of healing and reconnection.

With love,
Melanie

Dear Mom,

It's a beautiful morning on Old Screamer Mountain. This may be the first morning of my stay with no clouds whatsoever—just a slight haze hovering over the mountains in an otherwise pale blue sky. A perfect day for April's birthday. She's sixty-seven today. We talk by phone everyday—sometimes twice a day—but I'm really missing her on this special day.

Nancy cooked a sumptuous dinner for residency guests last night. She's a marvelous gourmet cook. Everything was meatless and every bit of it delicious. Because I'm trying to eat non-acidic foods, I had to go light on Nancy's home-grown tomato salad. But I devoured her creamy, light cheese soufflé, the perfectly browned and seasoned chunks of sweet potato, and the exquisite mixture of kale, summer squash, and goat cheese.

This dinner was a delightful and nurturing way to get acquainted with the other guests who have come to Old Screamer Mountain for solitude and writing. Kamla Dutt just arrived from Atlanta for her third stay here. She is in the Esther Cottage, next door to my Peeler Cottage. Kamla is a recently retired cancer researcher at the Morehouse School of Medicine. She is also an eminent Hindi poet, short story writer, and theater artist. She was deeply moved by the connections I have, through you and Dad, to this place and to Lillian Smith. And when I told her that you had developed some of the first courses in human sexuality ever taught at Michigan State University, she kept asking about you and your work throughout the dinner.

Nancy threw this dinner party in part to welcome Kamla and also to say goodbye to Pamela Best. Pamela is a poet, singer, songwriter, and spoken word artist who goes by the name of RareEpiphany when she performs. Her debut poetry collection, *Of Love*, was published last year. She lives in Atlanta with her son. After two weeks here on the mountain creating new work, Pamela is leaving tomorrow. Before the evening ended, Kamla and I prevailed upon Pamela to share one of her poems. She was magnificent!

Before parting I thanked Nancy and Robert for their gracious hospitality and commitment to keeping the rich history of Laurel Falls Camp alive and thriving. All three of us expressed (each in our own way) profound gratitude for the spacious psychic clearing and regenerative beauty we have found here.

It was a wonderful evening.

I'll write more soon,
Melanie

SUNDAY, JULY 22, 2012
Lillian E. Smith Center for the Arts
Old Screamer Mountain
Clayton, Georgia

Dear Mom,

At the end of the letter I wrote on Friday, I spoke of "the grace of dementia." You may have tripped over that phrase, wondering what in the world I was referring to. I'm not sure you would ever speak of dementia as "grace-filled." Even now, you visibly stiffen and scowl when I imply that your long- or short-term memory is not fully retrievable.

I suspect that you find dementia shameful. It's an assault on your competence and independence. I know from stories you've shared that excelling in school and extracurricular activities was a survival strategy you learned early in life. Later as a feminist, you were proudly noncompliant, strong-willed, and self-reliant. You took a lot of heat for that, especially as a pastor's wife in the 1950s. You were praised and greatly admired by others—a role model for countless women. As you aged you resented the assumption that you needed help and routinely rebuked those who offered. *I'm perfectly capable of carrying my own groceries!*

I understand your shame and fear. As I said yesterday, I feel a red-hot urgency to free up time for writing. I don't know how much time I have left before the advent of dementia. Some days I feel panic. And grief. Both have the power to wake me from a sound sleep in the middle of the night.

When this dread overtakes me, I want to remember what I've learned with you during the past eight years as your dementia has increased in severity. Yes, you have experienced devastating loss and decline. But dementia has also been the bearer of healing. We don't talk about any of this directly because you recoil at the mention of memory loss. Chances are I won't share this letter with you. I don't know. We'll see. But I need to name some of the gifts I have experienced. The remembering may later serve as antidote, especially when I descend into catastrophic fear.

To this day, Mom, your feisty spirit and humor remain intact. I can't tell you how many young caregivers at Burcham Hills have told me, "I hope I can be like your mother when I'm ninety years old. She's so much fun!"

And memory loss certainly hasn't destroyed your problem-solving capacities. You may not be able to reach back in time, but you make use of what is immediately at hand. Like last year when we were talking in your apartment and I announced that your ninetieth birthday was one month away.

"Are you sure?" you asked, looking highly doubtful. "How do you know that?"

"Because I've been your daughter for sixty-three years." I replied. Then, against my better judgment, I asked a remember question.

"Do you know how old you're going to be on May 21?"

You threw your head back and spit your words at me. "Yes, of course I know."

"How old?" I asked.

I waited while you scanned the apartment for clues. Neither of us moved. I wondered if I should rescue you by changing the subject. But then you looked directly at me and rolled your eyes as if any fool knows the answer.

"I'm going to be exactly ten years older than I was ten years ago!"

Later that day, I asked your permission to tell some of the other residents that you'd be turning ninety. You granted permission, but encouraged me to "check my facts," certain I'd gotten the age wrong. As we waited in the common area for lunch to be served, I solicited ideas from the women gathered for a really festive celebration of your upcoming ninetieth. Again you rolled your eyes.

"That's ridiculous," you said. "I'm not that old."

Margaret and Sally shot each other a glance and waited to see how I'd respond.

"So how old do you think you're going to be on May 21?" I asked.

I wasn't trying to humiliate you. You and I often teased each other in the presence of Margaret and Sally. We both knew how much they loved you. I also trusted that you'd flatly refuse to answer the question if you found it threatening.

"I was going to say fifty-five, but I think that's probably too young," you said.

"Yes," I confirmed, trying to stifle a smile. "Especially considering that I, your daughter, am sixty-three!"

You shrugged and waved your hand at me dismissively.

"We're not talking about *you*!"

As your dementia has grown more severe and self-reliance impossible, you still insist that your agency be respected at every turn. I love it that you don't hesitate to voice your dismay when people speak to you in a condescending tone. And I've seen a different side of you emerge, Mom. I've witnessed you giving and receiving affection as never before. You always thank caregivers for their thoughtfulness and you playfully call them "scamps." Your face lights up each and every time I walk through the door. When I ask how you're doing, you always reply, "Now that you're here, I'm just fine!"

Since you've been at Burcham, our physical intimacy has also deepened because you ask me to help you. To scratch your back. To slather your dry skin with lotion. To clip your nails. To help pull your sweater over your head. To unhook your bra. To pull your slacks up as you stand up from the toilet. Those are all intimate things to ask. And to give.

When you could still get around with the help of a walker, my favorite time to visit was after dinner in the early evening. The caregivers let me help you get undressed and into bed. Your first apartment was large enough for a double bed. After tucking you in, I'd lie next to you until you drifted into sleep. Lying on our backs, staring at the ceiling, we talked about random and unconnected subjects. The friend of yours I'd seen in the store that day. What April and I had eaten for dinner. The memories triggered by paintings and photographs hanging near the bed.

When you could no longer walk, you moved to a different floor and a smaller apartment with a hospital bed. You required two assists for getting to the bathroom or into bed, and I wasn't allowed to help. I changed my visiting time to earlier in the day so as not to disturb the caregivers' nighttime routines. The hospital bed wasn't wide enough for the two of us. It was one of the innumerable adjustments that had to be made, but I still miss those evening rituals.

And I'll never forget your very first night at Burcham in your original apartment. After you fell at home and came down with pneumonia. The doctors said it was unsafe for you to return home. Truman flew from Washington, DC. We found you a large studio apartment at Burcham. Then worked for twelve hours nonstop, packing your things and supervising the movers. We were hanging up the last of your clothes when the ambulance brought you to Burcham.

I slept the first three nights on a cot in your apartment. I didn't want you to wake in the morning frightened and disoriented.

You were so weak from ten days in the hospital you couldn't walk. I remember waking when light from the hallway flooded your room. A caregiver had come to take you to the bathroom. She asked you to put your arms around her neck while she lifted you from the bed and carried you into the bathroom. I was certain you'd resist or cry out in fear. The tenderness in your voice was unfamiliar: *Oh, thank you. Thank you. You are so gentle, so kind.*

I'd never seen you being carried, Mom. I don't know if your mother ever carried you. Or rocked you. Tucked you in. Cooed over you. Stroked your hair and face. Kissed you goodnight.

These are just some of the gifts, Mom. Of course there've been pain, struggle, and loss. But that's not the whole of it.

And I'm sick and tired of people who've known you for

years trying to console me with their pity. *It's so tragic what's happened to your mother. She was such a vital woman. It must be so hard on you. I'd go to see Eleanor, but I know she wouldn't remember me. . . .*

It takes every ounce of self-control not to scream, *How would you know? You haven't seen her in years!*

I suppress this rage because I, too, could very well have spoken those words to someone else if I hadn't been your intimate companion for the past decade. I also know that each person's journey with dementia is unique. The fact that you are still so present and very much yourself is not true of everyone with profound memory loss.

When people say such things about you, I tell them "tragic" isn't how I'd describe you. And being at Burcham isn't "a fate worse than death." I try to convey what I've learned from watching you interact with visitors.

It doesn't matter that my mother can't remember your name. Your presence will be a gift. She may not literally know who you are, but she will feel known by you. She'll know you share a common history. And that's what matters.

These last few years have been a healing time, after the hell we went through when I asked you to retire from Leaven. Wendy, Stephanie, and Truman can also testify to the healing they've experienced with you—each in their own way. I don't know what your experience has been, but I suspect there's been healing and grace for you as well.

Mom, during those endless months of impasse and estrangement between us, I sought the help of a therapist. I was despairing, fearing that you and I would never find our way through the pain and misunderstanding. My therapist said something during one of our sessions that I've never forgotten: "Life gives us at least two significant opportunities to heal from childhood wounds. *If* we seize those opportunities and become partners in the healing. It won't happen automatically, but it can happen. The first is when we have children of our own. The second is when caring for aging parents."

I haven't raised children of my own. But I'm privileged to be the child who lives closest to you. I'm grateful you've allowed me to care for you. I'm so thankful for all the precious times we've had since you moved to Burcham. That's what I mean by the grace of dementia.

Remembering all of this has caused me to change my mind. I want to read this letter to you. It wouldn't feel right to keep all of this to myself. Like everything else in these letters, this is history we share.

Love,
Melanie

Lillian E. Smith Center for the Arts
Old Screamer Mountain
Clayton, Georgia

Dear Mom,

This morning I remembered another time with you that will always be precious to me. It was a couple months ago. I stopped by to see you on a Saturday night after I had led a daylong workshop. You were already in bed but still awake. I bent over the bed rail. When you looked up at me, your face softened and you smiled broadly.

"Where'd you come from?" you asked, as if I hadn't been to see you the day before and the day before that.

"I just wanted to pop in and say goodnight." I pulled a chair close to the bed so I could hold your hand. We sat in silence as the light slowly faded in the room.

"Shall I put on some music, Mom?"

"Yes, that would be nice."

I found a Carolyn McDade CD that begins with the sounds of a heron calling out as it rises from a riverbed.

"Those are bird calls, Mom," I said, seeing you were puzzled by the sound. There was a time when you could have named the call of almost any bird.

"How did they get into the room?" you asked.

"There aren't any birds in the room, Mom. That's on a

record of Carolyn McDade songs. She often begins her songs with the sound of bird calls."

"Oh, yes. Of course," you said, pretending to remember.

When your eyelids narrowed, almost touching, you forced them open again. Turned to see if I was still here.

"Is it hard for you to listen to this music because it's so slow?" you asked.

"No. I find it very soothing, how about you?"

"Yes, it's beautiful." You squeezed my hand.

"Do you think you can sleep now if I leave, Mom?"

"Oh, I don't think so. I have much too much to remember," you said, trying to roll onto your left side to face me.

"What are you remembering?" I put another pillow behind your back to help you stay in that position. You pulled your right arm from under the quilt and motioned to the space between us.

"This time here with you."

"I'll stay a little longer," I said softly. You smiled, put your arm back under the cover, and closed your eyes.

When I thought you were asleep, I gently released your hand, but you opened your eyes.

"Mom, I need to go home now."

"Oh. Okay. Do you need me to convey something to anyone?" you asked, hoping to still be of some use in the world.

"No." I opened the door and the light from the hallway poured in. "There's no need to tell anyone anything tonight. You can just fall asleep now."

"Okay," you said and then added, "I wish I had a bigger bed."

I love you,
Melanie

JOURNAL ENTRY TUESDAY AFTERNOON, JULY 24, 2012

I STAYED UP late last night rereading the letters Lillian wrote in 1948 and 1949 explaining both why she felt compelled to write *Killers of the Dream* and how she found the courage and the strength to complete it. This afternoon I feel an urgency to go back and record quotes from those letters and from *Killers of the Dream* that I found particularly striking and moving.

Lillian started writing *Killers* four years after *Strange Fruit* took the country by storm. She was proud of having written that interracial love story and equally proud of the controversy it stoked. In 1946 she was working on another novel and had even signed a contract with a publisher. But she set that manuscript aside, convinced it was time for a white person to write a nonfiction account of the immeasurable devastation that white supremacy, white culture, and segregation continued to wreak. She believed all three were dream killers and she wanted to describe with forthright honesty and precision how that dream killing occurs.

I am grateful that Margaret Rose Gladney (the editor of the collected letters) mined Lillian's private, autobiographical notes about writing *Killers*. They reveal that she struggled mightily with finding the right voice and genre for this new book. Lillian says she wasted six to eight months trying to write a historical analysis in a dispassionate voice. The structure and purpose of *Killers* became clear only when she chose instead to write in a personal, passionate, and confessional voice.[11]

I deeply resonate with her struggle. I've been wrestling every day in this cottage with how I, as a white woman, should write about the horror of lynching. And whether it is even appropriate to write about the trauma that white children may have experienced at lynchings when those brutal desecrations left Black children fatherless and motherless.

Even though her writing began to flow when she made the choice to write autobiographically, Lillian described *Killers* as "the hardest of all books for me to write; it stirred deep and dangerous memories."[12] She also suspected this book would be met with resounding negative criticism by white people who prided themselves on being very liberal and progressive when it came to "race relations."

As I was reading how Lillian struggled with finding the right voice for this book and fearing that its highly personal, confessional genre would unleash severe criticism and rage in white readers, I recalled Nancy's words to me in the Common Room kitchen: "When you're excavating the deep interior terrain as you're doing and as Lil did, it's a cold corridor that you walk." And, "Lil had Paula. She had friends near and far. She corresponded daily with people who expressed love and support. Still, she battled loneliness."

I am so grateful that Lillian was willing to endure the loneliness, wade into deep waters, and confront those dangerous memories head-on. She held up a mirror to white people throughout the country, not only in the South. And that mirror still holds. I feel it every time I read *Killers*. I am in awe of the courage and candor she displayed as she unearthed white secrets and lies. Like those that fomented lynchings. She punctured white silence about the rampant sexual assault and rape of Black women by white men. And then she described in vivid detail how those white perpetrators sought to protect themselves by projecting their own sexual violence onto Black men. I want to record—for myself—just one example of this boldness that I read again last night:

> In the name of *sacred womanhood,* of *purity,* of *preserving the home,* lecherous old men and young ones, reeking with impurities, had violated the home since they were sixteen years old, whipped up lynchings, organized Klans, burned crosses, aroused the poor and ignorant to wild excitement by an obscene, perverse imagery describing the "menace" of Negro men hiding behind every cypress waiting to rape "our" women. In the name of such holiness, they did these things to keep the affairs of their own heart and conscience and home, as well as the community, "under control."[13]

Lillian had a foreboding about the avalanche of criticism that was bound to come. She also feared that *Killers* would hurt people she loved. She had written very personally about the lessons of sin, sex, and segregation that white children learned in their families. I cannot count the number of times I have read the chapter called "The Lessons." With searing precision and honesty, she describes dangerous memories like these in that chapter:

By the time we were five years old we had learned, without hearing the words, that masturbation is wrong and segregation is right, and each had become a dread taboo that must never be broken. . . . Wrapped together, [these lessons] were taught us by our mother's voice, memorized with her love, patted into our lives as she rocked us to sleep or fed us.[14]

It's no wonder then that Lillian wrote a letter to her family in October 1949, letting them know she had just mailed a copy of *Killers* to each of them and saying,

It is written as honestly as I know how to write. This honesty will hurt many people. I hope it does not hurt my own family too much. I am neither young enough nor old enough to be uncaring of the effect of my writings on the people I love. I hope that none of you will be too deeply embarrassed by my candor nor injured too much in your own work because of it. There will be much criticism. . . . Perhaps you can ignore it or perhaps you will remember that every one who suggests that profound change is necessary is always bitterly attacked.[15]

It's also no wonder that Lillian decided to close Laurel Falls Camp. She wrote the campers and parents, saying she'd been extraordinarily busy working on two books. She also revealed that she'd been suffering from a prolonged infection that left her exhausted. She did not mention her fear that the imminent publication of *Killers* might be too threatening for the parents of her campers.

I'm still not clear how Lillian was able to navigate the tensions that must have arisen in earlier years with disgruntled parents who disapproved of the "radical notions" their daughters brought home from camp. She must have walked a fine line at times in the letters she sent to parents explaining that Laurel Falls counselors did not shy away from honest discussion about controversial issues like lynching and segregation. She herself expressed surprise that parents kept sending their girls to Laurel Falls, year after year. In 1943, after a spate of newspaper and magazine articles had been published about her, she wrote a friend saying, "The odd thing is that with all this radical publicity about me, I have more campers . . . than I have ever had in the history of the camp. . . . It is a strange, queer world." [16]

It astounds me that the publication of *Strange Fruit* did not result in a drastic drop in camper enrollment. It was a radical book when it appeared in 1944. And its release was no secret. One million copies of the hardback edition were sold. It went through two printings and was translated into fifteen different languages. When it was banned in Boston and Detroit, due to its "lewd language," Lillian showed no inclination to close Laurel Falls. But five years later she could not imagine having the physical or emotional stamina needed to weather a more severe controversy while also running the camp.

The decision to close Laurel Falls was agonizing for Lillian. She was fifty-one years old. She had devoted half her life to making Laurel Falls a highly innovative camp. She loved the work and she loved the campers. Her grief is evident in the letter she wrote to the parents on March 21, 1949:

Twenty-eight years of memories are hard to close the door on. To tell myself that this experience of growing up with children is over, is a thing impossible to do. So impossible that I have to keep a crack in the door by whispering, "Maybe we can have camp again next summer." But I know, and I think you know, that closing camp this summer will write "finish" to this chapter of my life that has been rich and creative and sweet and good. . . . I hope the idea of Laurel Falls will not die. I want to believe that we have started a chain reaction of dreams that will go on touching child after child in our South.[17]

Here I am on Old Screamer Mountain, five months after the Leaven Center board, by necessity, has closed the door on seventeen years of rich, creative, sweet, and good memories. And I still find it impossible to tell myself that this dream has ended.

∾

Peeler Cottage at the Lillian E. Smith Center

*Chimney adjacent to Lillian Smith's grave marker
at the Lillian E. Smith Center*

Lillian E. Smith Center for the Arts
Old Screamer Mountain
Clayton, Georgia

Dear Mom,

Every few days I stop to talk with Lillian by the old stone chimney. Especially when I wrestle with self-doubt. I ask her how she stayed the course. How she withstood the "demon voices" that tried to distract and derail her. I know she was dismayed and at times distraught by the harsh criticism that *Killers of the Dream* received when it first appeared. She had little regard for Ralph McGill, senior editor of the *Atlanta Constitution*, but his scathing reviews of *Killers* must have stung, knowing that many white liberals regarded him as a beacon of progressive change in the South.

McGill heaped scorn upon *Killers of the Dream*, calling it "strident" and dismissing it as the private agony of a deranged soul: "Miss Smith is a prisoner in the monastery of her own mind. But rarely does she come out of its gates, and then, apparently, seeing only wicked things to send her back to her hair shirt and the pouring of ashes on her head and salt in her own psychiatric wounds."[18]

I ask Lillian how she protected herself against such violent onslaughts. How she stayed rooted in her vision and found the courage to name what needed to be named. Here I am seven decades later, wrestling mightily with self-doubt, trying to withstand the voices that keep intruding, hurling question after question at me.

This morning I was overcome with panic and anticipatory grief. I have only three more days on this mountain. So much remains unwritten. Returning home to Michigan, my other work will inevitably take precedence again. Solitude will be hard won. Unsettled at the thought of saying goodbye to my precious mountain hermitage, I decided to visit Lillian's grave once again.

The ground was wet and spongy from an afternoon cloudburst, so I remained standing at the grave, although I have often kneeled. Thunder could be heard crackling down a distant mountainside.

"I need your companionship, Lillian, as I prepare to leave this sacred place. If you could just let me know you're with me, every now and again, I'd be so grateful."

I took a photo of the metal marker and another of the old stone chimney. Then turned back toward the cottage in hopes of finishing an essay I'd been working on for the past three days.

I'd just settled into the blue, flowered armchair when my cell phone buzzed from the windowsill. It was Shayla Griffin. Shayla's the colleague I've told you about, Mom. She and I have been facilitating anti-racism workshops for K–12 teachers. She was calling to check in about a workshop we're leading next month.

She asked how my writing was going and if I was making any progress on the lynching project. I responded, "It's been an emotional roller coaster, but I'm incredibly grateful for these three weeks of solitude and writing."

"Have I ever told you what I wanted to do for my senior thesis at Spelman?" Shayla asked.

"I don't think so," I said. I knew Shayla had graduated from Spelman College in 2005, but I didn't know anything about her senior thesis.

"I wanted to interview white people who'd been forced by their parents to witness lynchings. You know . . . those three- and four-year-olds who were hoisted up on their parents' shoulders so they could get a better look. That must've been incredibly traumatic."

I stopped pacing the cottage floor and stared out the window, unable to absorb the magnitude of what just happened. As I struggled to find words, Shayla continued.

"My professor sat me down. He asked, how would I find these old white people? And why would they want to talk with me? I didn't have good answers. So I abandoned the project."

"Shayla," I said, still groping for words, "this is remarkable. That's what I'm trying to write about. Those white children. The trauma they must have experienced. I can't believe we've never talked about this before."

"Wow! That's amazing. I'm so glad you're doing that."

"Thanks," I replied. "But I'm so often riddled with doubts. Just knowing you wanted to write about this encourages me."

"At the time," Shayla said, "I didn't understand why my professor was being so hard on me. Later it made sense. He was trying to tell me: that's not my work as a Black woman. But it is your work, Melanie."

After hanging up, I sat for a long time, Mom, letting the

stillness of the cottage hold and extend the wonder of that conversation. I could hardly move. I made a cup of Bengal Spice tea—the flavor you loved so much you always bought five or six boxes at a time, so you'd never run out. I held the warmth with both hands and inhaled the cinnamon, ginger, and roasted chicory. Then I knew I had to write you and tell you what happened.

With love and awe,
Melanie

Lillian E. Smith Center for the Arts
Old Screamer Mountain
Clayton, Georgia

Dear Mom,

Why does it happen that certain questions surface and become so urgent only after a person dies? I assumed for years that I knew everything I needed to know about Dad's departure from the South. He was such a good storyteller, and he frequently regaled us with stories about Birmingham, Alabama, his father's segregationist worldview, and the events that converged in his youth and caused him to begin critically reassessing everything he had been taught about race.

But it wasn't until two years after his death, while on my three-month sabbatical in North Carolina, that a torrent of new questions came gushing to the fore in me:

Exactly when, how, and why did Dad begin to question segregation? What were the precipitating events?

Who did he confide in as his world began to crack open and he felt a growing sense of estrangement from his family?

Before he got to college, did he have any other people in his life besides his pastor, Henry Edmonds, who raised critical questions about racism and racial violence and modeled for him a different way of being white?

These are just a few of the questions that emerged during those three months in North Carolina in 2008. Each new question unlocked more, but it was too late to ask him. And I couldn't ask you because, by that time, you could retrieve very few memories from those early years with Dad.

Why had I never thought to ask Dad these questions when he was alive? I can't account for the timing. I just know it would have been a whole lot easier if I had. Now I'm left trying to fit pieces of a puzzle together with few people able to validate my hunches or discern the pattern with me.

I've been working all day on an essay called "Soul Splitting." I am trying to describe the trauma-induced dissociation that may have occurred in white children who were brought to lynchings, forced to watch, and sometimes compelled to participate in grizzly acts of torture.

If I could talk with Dad, I would ask him whether his father, "Poppy," ever spoke of witnessing this kind of racial violence as a child.

I'd also ask Dad to tell me about his grandfather, John Morrison. I don't remember Dad ever talking about his grandparents, which seems very strange to me because he must have known them. They lived only a few miles from Mountain Brook, in Ensley—a community adjacent to Birmingham. Because I know so little about Poppy's father and mother, I have no idea whether they would have taken their sons to lynchings as a ritualistic rite of passage into white manhood.

What I do know is this: my research has revealed that by the time Poppy was fifteen years old, ten Black men had been lynched within a fifteen-mile radius of the two Alabama towns where he lived—Blocton and Ensley.

Ten human beings wrenched from their families—hunted down, abducted, and brutalized. Ten Black men, survived by spouses and children, mothers and fathers, sisters and brothers. Ten acts of terrorism inflicted on an entire Black community in those towns. Ten horrific murders that left Black families and communities physically and emotionally scarred for generations.

These were the ten lynchings in that area reported in Alabama newspapers between 1893 and 1909. The actual number of victims is likely greater. In that same time period, 175 Black men statewide were lynched and hundreds more in neighboring states.

Even if Poppy was never physically present at a lynching, the reality of lynching was stitched into the fabric of everyday life in his Alabama childhood and adolescence. In 1892, the year before Poppy's birth, more than 250 Black people were lynched throughout the United States—the highest number recorded for any single year.

White newspapers in the towns where he was raised frequently reported lynchings that occurred throughout the state and the region, often replete with graphic details of how the victim died. It is very likely that Poppy had friends who bragged that their family members had been to a lynching. He undoubtedly heard adults talking about a recent lynching, adding their commentaries about the precipitating offense, the impressive size of the crowd, or the fruitless pleading of the victim.

Dad always told us he believed that alcoholism and the devastating impact of the Depression provoked Poppy's episodic abuse and rage. Maybe so, but I have to wonder if there were other sources of pain that he was numbing with alcohol. Could it be that he had witnessed racial violence at the hands of trusted elders like schoolteachers, shopkeepers, deacons from his church, or family members? I'm not trying to argue for a one-dimensional causality, but I find it deeply disturbing that so few articles and books have examined what Toni Morrison calls "the severe fragmentation of self" that the trauma of racism caused in white people as well as people of color.[19] The grandfather I came to know through Dad's stories was most definitely a man whose soul was fragmented.

And I'm asking these questions because I believe it's incumbent on us as white people to examine how the attitudes, practices, prejudices, and traumas of white supremacy have been passed down through generations. The legacies of white supremacy continue to live in us, at a cellular level, despite our protestations to the contrary. Lillian knew this. She described it flawlessly in *Killers of the Dream*:

> What white southerner of my generation ever stops to think consciously where to go or asks himself if it is right to go there! His muscles know where he can go and take him to the front of the streetcar, to the front of the bus, to the big school, to the hospital, to the library, to hotel and restaurant and picture show, into the best that his town has to offer its citizens. These ceremonials in honor of white supremacy, performed since babyhood, slip from the conscious mind down deep into muscles and glands and become difficult to tear out.[20]

Writing to a friend years later about *Killers of the Dream*, Lillian said: "I wrote it because I had to find out what life in a segregated culture had done to me."[21]

The segregated culture that Lillian knew has changed but it isn't dead. Its legacies are still present in what Michelle

Alexander calls the New Jim Crow of mass incarceration, racial profiling, police violence, and voter suppression. I'm on this mountain, Mom, researching and writing about the intergenerational legacy of lynching and white supremacy because unless and until we, as white Americans, acknowledge and confront the psychic, emotional and spiritual legacies of this horrific history, we will continue to project—consciously or unconsciously—racialized fears, fantasies, rage, and scapegoating onto people of color.

Here's what I say in my essay about the urgency of acknowledging and confronting the legacies of lynching:

> It is long past time that those of us who are white demand a truthful accounting of who is actually in mortal danger in this country. It is long past time that those of us who are white bring our collective hearts, minds, and souls to the task of excavating, naming, and untying this lethal knot of fear that resides in white imaginations. This knot has many threads— each one an unacknowledged legacy of white supremacy, enslaving, and lynching. In this lethal knot, there are threads of fear of Black and brown bodies; there are threads that seek to protect white-only space and curtail the free movement by people of color; there are threads of rage at so-called insubordination; there are threads of white people feeling small and afraid even when they're armed with assault weapons.

I agree with Shayla. It is not the work of Black people to unearth, untie, and disarm this lethal knot of white supremacist consciousness that remains so deeply rooted and endemic in our white psyches. It is white people's work. We must do this work in every relationship and vocation at our disposal—as parents, friends, co-workers, neighbors, and citizens of this nation.

I hope to God we will.

Love,
Melanie

Lillian E. Smith Center for the Arts
Old Screamer Mountain
Clayton, Georgia

Dear Mom,

This afternoon I decided to venture out and go hunting for
the remnants of Laurel Falls Camp. I knew that some of the
buildings had been destroyed by fire and others had been
purposely demolished because of age, but I hoped to find the
old swimming hole or what used to be the tennis courts and
riding stables. I wanted to take pictures of places where you
might have walked, played, eaten, or read.

As I walked the gravel road that snakes around the mountain, I found no detours that led anywhere or appeared to be
trails. On both sides of the road, all I could see were woods,
until I came upon a stairway of maybe fifty large stone,
moss-covered steps leading to the crest of a hill. I climbed
that dark green stairway with great anticipation, expecting
to come upon relics of Laurel Falls. At the top I found only
more trees and a narrow deer path leading down the mountain. Disappointed and defeated, I headed back to my cottage. On the road I ran into Robert, who was walking Bailey,
his little white Jack Russell terrier.

"Where in the world did the girls ride horses around here
or play tennis and badminton?" I asked. "All I see are woods
and more woods. Where are the old buildings?"

"Most everything has been demolished," Robert told me. "I can show you where the courts and riding range used to be and where the dining hall stood. Aside from a few woods that he spared, the entire mountain had been clear-cut by Lillian's father."

"You mean it was bald?" I asked. "It's hard to imagine with such dense forests now."

"Everything you see here is second growth," he said.

"Well, that solves the mystery. The photograph of the campers in the Common Room shows the girls standing on what appears to be a prairie."

"Yes," he said, shaking his head. "I don't know why Grandfather Smith obliterated the forests like that."

Coming back to my cottage, I felt unsettled and restless. It was as if something were weighing on my spirit, but I could not pinpoint the source of the heaviness. In the course of the afternoon, my sadness deepened. I wanted to cry but tears wouldn't come. I can't say for sure when or why it gradually dawned on me that my grief about the Leaven Center's demise had been awakened on that search for the remnants of Laurel Falls.

I wanted to call you to talk about it. And then realized I couldn't.

My morning walk on the mountain had thrown me back to last October when the board announced that the Leaven Center would be closing in late January. I so hoped the center would continue to serve future generations.

People tried to comfort me during the depths of my grief by saying, "Leaven isn't dying! It will live on in the thousands of people who came through that special place and were transformed by it. The spirit of Leaven can't die." Like a widow who finds no comfort in talk of immortality, I coveted the body as well as the spirit of my beloved Leaven. After all, they are conjoined. Leaven Center programs were anchored in a particular, wholly unique place on the earth, with a distinctive bend in the river, irreplaceable spruce trees in front of the lodge, and an uncommonly deep gorge created by the inexhaustible waters of that spring-fed stream.

There is a sacramental significance to places like Laurel Falls and the Leaven Center. The transformation and community that people found at Laurel Falls and Leaven are inseparable from the sights and smells and sounds of the land. The attachment people feel for those centers is a bodily thing, tactile and sensual. Even when a Laurel Falls camper or a Leaven Center guest never returned in person, the fact that those places continued to exist brought them solace and hope.

That's why I was so heartsick and adrift for months after the decision was announced last October. I couldn't bear the thought of that "thin" holy place no longer being in the world as Leaven. It made no sense that so many people had poured their time, energy, love, and resources into creating that glorious experiment only to have it come to an end.

As I've told you, Mom, when I was leading groups at Leaven last fall, after the announcement and before the closing ceremony, it was excruciating. Everywhere I turned, there were memories and associations. We put so much love and care into choosing the comforters on the beds, the plates on the table, the rugs on the floors, and the paintings on the walls. What will become of all these precious things, I wondered? They belong *here*.

I can't imagine how Lillian and Paula found the resolve or courage to remove those decaying camp buildings whose rafters had absorbed the laughter and stories of so many teen-age girls. Did they leave the mountain when the demolition crew was working or stay and watch, holding each other up?

Over those intense and interminable months of grieving, I was consoled by April's conviction that the land is stronger than any of us who have lived there; it will survive and out-live us all. I strained to see the long view and let its wisdom carry me. I also found comfort during my visits with you, Mom. We didn't talk much about the closing of the Leaven Center, but you could see I was tired, and you invited me to stretch out on your couch. I had such trouble sleeping at night for months, but I frequently drifted off to sleep on your couch, with you sitting nearby. You were so sweet to me. When I came to again, I felt chagrined for being such poor company, but you waved aside my apologies and said, "I'm so glad you could sleep. You needed it. Do you want to spend the night?"

With time, the tidal waves of grief subsided, decreasing in force and intensity as I struggled to find my way back to the life I had chosen when I left Leaven. Then unexpectedly, in place of the potential buyers who wanted to rip out the meeting room and dispose of the ramp, Laura Apol decided to purchase the lodge. Isn't it amazing, Mom? Laura, who has been a supporter of the Leaven Center since the found-ing, and who led writing workshops at the center every win-ter. She is bringing her own dreams to the lodge, and also brings firsthand knowledge of Leaven's history on that land. She honors the fact that she stands in a long line of people who have cherished that land. After the sale, Laura said she felt the word *steward* was fitting, considering what has been entrusted to her care.

Here I sit, four weeks after that sale was consummated, on the porch of the Peeler Cottage watching a thunderstorm move through the mountains. When I returned from my conversation with Robert, I looked up the definition of "second growth" and learned that it is a forest that has regrown after a major disturbance such as fire, infestation, or timber harvest.

Last summer when I applied to come here, I had no idea that the Leaven Center would soon be closing. Nor did I imagine that Old Screamer Mountain would have so much to teach me about the never-ending cycles of holding on and letting go. This mountain that sustained clear-cutting and numerous fires is now lush with vegetation. Buildings that once housed teenage girls are places of respite and solitude for writers and artists. Nancy and Robert are taking painstaking care to discern, with the Lillian Smith Foundation board, the way forward: a way that will protect this mountain, honor its rich history, and welcome the advent of change. And in Michigan, the Leaven Center Lodge that welcomed thousands of people over the course of its twelve-year history is being remade and readied for its next incarnation.

I knew I needed to come here, Mom. I just didn't know the half of why. With each passing day on this mountain, I've felt my body and spirit healing. Tomorrow, I leave for home. I think it's safe to say that I may be ready for a season of second growth.

Love,
Melanie

SUNDAY, JULY 29, 2012
Lillian E. Smith Center for the Arts
Old Screamer Mountain
Clayton, Georgia

Dear Mom,

It's 10:00 a.m. and I'm preparing to leave this sacred mountain. I've eaten my usual breakfast of oatmeal with dried cherries and brown sugar. I took my final morning walk in the hills at Rabun County Park. The workspace has been disassembled. The mighty cloud of witnesses securely packed for safe travel. My suitcases and crates of books are in the car.

I'll stop to give Nancy and Robert the keys on the way out. And thank them profusely for their extravagant hospitality, their exquisite care for this land, and their steadfast devotion to the legacy Lillian and Paula birthed here.

Last week, I reread the letter Lillian wrote to parents in the wake of her agonizing decision to close Laurel Falls: "I hope that the idea of Laurel Falls will not die. I want to believe that we have started a chain reaction of dreams that will go on touching child after child in our South."[22]

That was an ambitious dream! And yet Lillian couldn't begin to foresee all the people she and this place would touch for generations to come. Including you, Mom, and through you—me.

I leave this mountain more convinced than ever that those of us who are white must critically examine and interrupt the intergenerational legacies that white supremacy has bequeathed us. As Lillian noted, the practices, fears, and fantasies of white supremacy have long ago slipped from our conscious minds into our muscles, glands, sinews, and imaginations. Excavating and eradicating this legacy will require deep, sustained, and unflinching work.

I leave this mountain humbled and emboldened. I've learned that every place is inhabited, by spirits known and unknown to us. We are the heirs of so many who have dreamed and prayed and risked on our behalf—whether we know it or not. What we set in motion will touch so many more than we can ever imagine. And yet none of us are in control of what will perish and what will remain.

I'm grateful to you and Dad for the intentionality and care you took to pay homage to your spiritual ancestors. Thank you for hanging their photographs on the wall, reading aloud from their poems and essays, and sharing stories of how they inspired your passion for justice. I might not otherwise have encountered Lillian Smith or felt compelled to continue the work she'd begun. I might never have come to this mountain or written these letters.

And speaking of letters, I leave this mountain with thirteen letters addressed to you! I plan to select sections from the letters to read aloud when I see you. I'll be home mid-afternoon on Monday. I'll stop by Burcham first thing. I can't wait to see you!

With love,
Melanie

*Walkway leading to the Esther and Peeler Cottages
at the Lillian E. Smith Center*

Burcham Hills Retirement Community
East Lansing, Michigan

MOTHER WAS IN her room, asleep in the wheelchair, her head resting on the palm of her hand. She was wearing the pale blue sweater that so perfectly matched her eyes, a string of colored beads, and as always a pair of dark blue knit pants.

"Hi, Mom," I said bending down to softly announce my presence.

She jerked awake and blinked several times, trying to bring my face into focus. Dread shot through me: maybe I have been gone too long and she won't know me anymore.

"Oh, hi. I'm so glad to see you." Her tenderness allowed me to exhale.

"I'm so happy to see you, Mom. I've missed you terribly."

I probably should have sat for a while, talking about nothing in particular, just letting the sight of me on her flowered couch reassure her. But I was eager to share the letters.

"I've just returned from Georgia where I was staying in a center for writers, just a few hours from where you went to college, Mom." I paused, waiting for the word "college" to spark recognition. She could not recall the names of her grandchildren, but the name of her alma mater was always retrievable.

"You mean Wesleyan College in Macon, Georgia?"

"Yes, Wesleyan College. You told me years ago that one of your favorite professors at Wesleyan took you and a small group of students up to North Georgia to Laurel Falls Camp to spend the weekend with Lillian Smith and Paula Snelling."

Mother nodded as if remembering, but I was doubtful. I had read somewhere that long-term memories can be triggered by sensory details, so I plied her with visual images of the camp.

"Laurel Falls was on a mountain in the Blue Ridge Mountains. It had riding horses, tennis courts, a swimming hole, and an indoor theater."

"Oh, yes," she said with confidence. I fell for it because I wanted to believe she could remember, that we could do this as a team.

"How would you describe the camp, Mom, and the time you spent there?"

"You mean . . . did it go well?"

"Yes, did it go well? What the place was like? What do you remember about Lillian Smith?" I wanted to name all the options before dementia descended again like thick mountain fog.

"Well, as you can see from up here, the place looks like it's collapsed on one side." She was pointing at the painting on the wall behind me.

"Mom, I was wondering if you remember Laurel Falls Camp where you met Lillian Smith and Paula Snelling."

"Well, sort of," she said, still examining the painting of dilapidated houses in a mountain valley. "Next to the collapsed house, there's a teeny thing that isn't particularly important. I can't tell what it is right now. At this moment, I don't remember it."

I so hoped the mention of Laurel Falls and Old Screamer Mountain would be triggers. And they may have been. She successfully located the only object in her apartment remotely related to mountains. I decided to move to a different chair and turn her wheelchair away from the painting.

"Mom, I just got back from spending three weeks in the Blue Ridge Mountains. I was staying at Laurel Falls Camp where Lillian Smith used to live and write." I said Lillian's first name slowly, accentuating all three syllables. "You visited Laurel Falls seventy-three years ago! You were eighteen years old."

"It's hard to believe I could have been *that* old."

"You were a student in college at the time."

"At Wesleyan College in Macon."

"Exactly. A professor took you and some other students up to North Georgia to visit Lillian Smith. She was a white Southerner who wrote scathing critiques of segregation and white supremacy."

Mother nodded again, reaching under the waistband of her slacks to scratch her lower back. For months, the geriatrician had been searching for clues to diagnose the source of her chronic itching but had come up empty-handed.

"I wrote you letters almost every day while I was in Georgia. But I didn't have a way to send them, so I brought them with me. I'd like to read one or two to you."

"Oh, you want to do that now?" she asked, twisting to the left to scratch behind her shoulder blade.

I opened the notebook and explained that I was going to read the first letter.

"Dear Mom, I'm here! On Old Screamer Mountain! I arrived yesterday mid-afternoon, having spent Saturday night with friends in Lexington, Kentucky. My heart started pounding as soon as—"

Mother interrupted. "I don't think I know where Lexington, Kentucky is." She lifted her blouse to scratch under her breasts. Her midriff was dark red and swollen.

"It's about halfway between Michigan and Georgia."

"Oh, that's right."

I continued reading. "My heart started pounding as soon as I saw the Lillian E. Smith Center sign decorated with a large hand-painted mountain laurel—"

"Could you scratch my back, just a little?"

"I will in a moment, Mom. I want to read this letter that I wrote you from Georgia."

"Could you read it while you scratch my back? Please?"

I laid the letters aside. Standing behind Mother's wheelchair, lifting her sweater and running the back of my fingernails across her shoulders, I told her that I had just returned from Georgia where I had stayed at a retreat center that used to be Laurel Falls Camp.

"You met Lillian Smith at Laurel Falls, Mom, seventy-three years ago, in 1939."

"That's a long time ago," Mother said, bending forward so I could reach further down her back.

"You were eighteen years old." I pulled her sweater down and returned to my seat.

"Years ago, Mom, you told me about that trip to Laurel

Falls Camp and meeting Lillian Smith. Going there was so important to you because Lillian Smith's writing had meant so much to you. Her novel *Strange Fruit* was published in 1944. It was very controversial because she wrote about an interracial relationship and lynching."

The novel's title seemed to spark recognition. Mother leaned toward me and narrowed her eyes as she listened.

"You're nodding like you remember *Strange Fruit.*"

"Yes," she said. "I mean I heard about it. I remember it was talked about and so forth."

I was delighted and not entirely surprised that she might remember the title of this novel. It created quite a sensation throughout the South.

"I'm so grateful that you and Dad introduced me to Lillian Smith's books. She's inspired my own writing, Mom, and I . . ."

"Please, Melanie, scratch my back," she pleaded, oblivious to my musings. "It would mean so much to me if you'd scratch my back."

I sat for a moment looking down at the letters. Then folded them and slid them into my bag.

"Let's take your sweater and bra off, Mom, so I can slather lotion on your back." She held her arms in the air to assist me. I wetted a cool hand towel and laid it on her hot shoulders. Then squirted lotion up and down her back and rubbed it in with strong circular motions.

"Oh, Melanie, that feels so good. That's exactly what I needed. Please don't stop. Please don't stop."

After patting baby powder into the thick blanket of lotion that stretched down the length of her back, I kneeled in front of her wheelchair and poured a pool of lotion into my hands. I asked her to hold up her breasts while I rubbed the lotion on her stomach. She had closed her eyes and didn't seem to hear me.

"Please hold your breasts up, Mom, so I can rub the lotion under them."

"Oh, sorry," she said, laughing. "I thought you asked me to hold my breath."

Both of us were laughing now. Mother playfully picked up one breast, then the other, and asked, "Is this what you want?"

I looked up at her and nodded.

"Yes, Mom, this is exactly what I want."

Lillian Smith's grave marker

Porch at the Peeler Cottage

ACKNOWLEDGMENTS

The writing of this book has been guided and sustained by an exceptionally generous and insightful circle of friends, colleagues, writers and family members. I am profoundly grateful for their professional, emotional, material and spiritual support.

To those who believed in this project when it first took flight, I am deeply grateful: Demetria Martinez, Nancy Smith Fichter, Laura Apol, Marcella Pendergrass, Lois McCullen Parr, Emily Joye McGaughy, Preston Van Vliet, Shayla Griffin, Tama Hamilton-Wray, Lisa Laughman and Karen Pace.

During different stages of writing, I benefitted from the wisdom, expertise and encouragement of trusted readers whose thoughtful and meticulous feedback helped make this a stronger and better book: Joanne Abel, Monique Savage, Pat Barnes-McConnell, Emily Joye McGaughy, Nan Jackson, Laura Apol, Autumn Joy LeBlanc Campbell, Naomi Ortiz, Robert Corley, Teresa Barnes, Jennifer Harvey, Lois McCullen Parr, Tama Hamilton-Wray, Susie Shaffer, and Robert Williams.

I am indebted to my siblings—Truman, Wendy, and Stephanie—for their careful reading of the manuscript and their affirmation that I have done justice to the remarkable woman who birthed and mothered us.

I will be forever grateful to Lillian Smith's niece, Nancy Smith Fichter, and her husband Robert Fichter, who for years came to North Georgia each summer from Tallahassee to oversee the residency program and lovingly care for the Lillian E. Smith Center. It was an enormous privilege to spend many hours with Nancy and Robert during my first two residencies on Old Screamer Mountain. I am also grateful for the exquisite hospitality bestowed on every Lillian E. Smith Center guest by those who greeted us and cared for the land and cottages: John Siegel, John Templeton, Pearl Fortson and Bill Watts. It brings me great joy to know that the rich offerings of the Lillian E. Smith Center continue to flourish under the stewardship of Piedmont College and the accomplished leadership of Matthew Teutsch.

The generous and skillful team who produced this book deserves high praise: Jeanette Stokes, for her indomitable spirit and innovative leadership of RCWMS; Bonnie Campbell for her beautiful book design; Marcy Litle, Rebecca Welper, and Rachel Sauls for their careful handling of the book, including editing and proofreading.

My wise and gifted spouse, April Allison, always believed that these letters should be shared with the world. She, most of all, is deserving of my thanks. When I grew discouraged, or feared these letters might be too idiosyncratic, she shook her head and told me to get back to work. When I emerged from my study with renewed enthusiasm and asked if I could read the latest section aloud to her, she was there to receive me. With pen in hand, she offered exceptional editorial feedback every step of the way. And her love, as always, kept me grounded and able to carry on.

Finally, I thank Lillian E. Smith and Eleanor S. Morrison for the manifold gifts they brought to this world, the tenacious courage they embodied, and the rich legacies they left us.

Stone stairway at the Lillian E. Smith Center
on Old Screamer Mountain

NOTES

1. Lillian Smith, *How Am I to Be Heard?: Letters of Lillian Smith*, ed. Margaret Rose Gladney (Chapel Hill: University of North Carolina Press, 1993), 75.

2. Smith, *To Be Heard*, 23.

3. Lillian Smith, "Human in Bondage," in *The Winner Names the Age: A Collection of Writings by Lillian Smith*, ed. Michele Cliff (New York: W. W. Norton), 34.

4. Lillian Smith, "The Moral and Political Significance of the Students' Non-Violent Protests," in *The Winner Names the Age: A Collection of Writings by Lillian Smith*, ed. Michele Cliff (New York: W. W. Norton), 96.

5. Lillian Smith, *Killers of the Dream*, reissued ed. (1949; repr., New York: W. W. Norton, 1994), 97–98.

6. Smith, *To Be Heard*, 106.

7. Smith, 106.

8. Margaret Rose Gladney, "Lillian Smith's Hope for Southern Women," *Southern Studies* 22, no. 3 (1983): 274–84.

9. Sherrilyn A. Ifill, *On the Courthouse Lawn: Confronting the Legacy of Lynching in the Twenty-First Century* (Boston: Beacon Press, 2008), viii.

10. Ifill, *On the Courthouse Lawn*, xi.

11. Smith, *To Be Heard*, 115.

12. Smith, 115.

13. Smith, *Killers of the Dream*, 145.

14. Smith, 83–84.

15. Smith, *To Be Heard*, 127.

16. Smith, 74.

17. Smith, 123–124.

18. Smith, 129.

19. Toni Morrison, "Unspeakable Things Unspoken," in *The Source of Self-Regard, Selected Speeches, Essays and Meditations* (New York: Alfred A. Knopf, 2019), 177.

20. Smith, *Killers of the Dream*, 96.

21. Smith, 13.

22. Smith, *To Be Heard*, 124.

BOOKS BY LILLIAN SMITH

Strange Fruit 1944

Killers of the Dream 1949

The Journey 1954

Now Is the Time 1955

One Hour 1959

Memory of a Large Christmas 1962

Our Faces, Our Words 1964

The Winner Names the Age: A Collection of Writings 1978
(edited by Michelle Cliff)

How Am I to Be Heard?: Letters of Lillian Smith 1993
(edited by Margaret Rose Gladney)

A Lillian Smith Reader 2016
(edited by Margaret Rose Gladney and Lisa Hodgens)

BOOKS BY ELEANOR S. MORRISON

Creative Teaching in the Church 1963
(Virgil E. Foster, co-author)

Growing Up in the Family: A Family Resource Book 1964
(Truman A. Morrison, co-author)

Human Sexuality: Contemporary Perspectives 1973
(Vera Borsage, co-editor)

Values in Sexuality: A New Approach to Sex Education 1974
(Mila Underhill Price, co-author)

Growing Up Sexual 1980
(Kay Starks, Cynda Hyndman, and Nina Ronzio, co-authors)

*Created in God's Image: A Human Sexuality Program for Ministry
and Mission* 1993
(Melanie S. Morrison, co-author)

Growing Up Sexual (Second Edition) 1996
(Kay Johnson Starks, co-author)

MELANIE S. MORRISON is the author of four books, including *Murder on Shades Mountain: The Legal Lynching of Willie Peterson and the Struggle for Justice in Jim Crow Birmingham*. As a racial justice educator, she has thirty years of experience designing and facilitating transformational group process. She served as executive director of Allies for Change, a national network of anti-oppression educators, and as director of the Leaven Center, a retreat and study center in Michigan dedicated to nurturing the relationship between spirituality and social justice. In 1994 she co-founded Doing Our Own Work, an intensive anti-racism program for white people that has attracted hundreds of participants across the country. She has a master of divinity from Yale Divinity School and a PhD from the University of Groningen in the Netherlands. She lives in Okemos, Michigan with her beloved spouse, April Allison.